STORAGE PROJECTS

◆ YOU CAN BUILD ◆

THE WEEKEND PROJECT BOOK SERIES

Storage Projects You Can Build, by David & Jeanie Stiles
Woodworking Simplified, by David & Jeanie Stiles
Garden Projects You Can Build, by David & Jeanie Stiles
Kids' Furniture You Can Build, by David & Jeanie Stiles
Playhouses You Can Build, by David & Jeanie Stiles

STORAGE PROJECTS
• YOU CAN BUILD •

DAVID & JEANIE STILES

WITH ILLUSTRATIONS
BY DAVID STILES

CHAPTERS™

CHAPTERS PUBLISHING LTD., SHELBURNE, VERMONT 05482

Published by Chapters Publishing Ltd.
2085 Shelburne Road
Shelburne, Vermont 05482

Library of Congress Cataloging-in-Publication Data
Stiles, David R.
Storage projects you can build / David & Jeanie Stiles; with illustrations by
David Stiles.
    p.   cm — (The Weekend project book series)
Includes index.
ISBN 1-57630-017-X (pbk.)
1. Woodwork. 2. Storage in the home.
I. Stiles, Jeanie. II. Title. III. Series: Stiles, David R. Weekend project book series
TT185.S738 1996
684.104—dc20
          96-32688

Printed and bound in Canada by Webcom

Book design by Eugenie Seidenberg Delaney
Photography by Skip Hine

FRONT COVER ACCESSORIES:
Ficus Tree and Begonia Plant—Wittendale's Florist & Greenhouses, Inc., 89 Newtown Ln.,
East Hampton, NY 11937, 516-324-7160; *Kitchen Utensils*—Sylvester & Co., Main St.,
Sag Harbor, NY 11963, 516-725-5012; *Lamp, Armchair & Rug*—English Country Antiques,
P.O. 1995, Snake Hollow Rd., Bridgehampton, NY 11932, 516-537-0606, and
English Country Antiques, 21 Newtown Ln., East Hampton, NY 11937, 516-329-5773.

All designs by the author, unless otherwise noted.

To our daughter, Lief Anne,
who continues to amaze us with her
accomplishments and creativity.

Acknowledgments

MANY THANKS TO Darcy and Richard Bockman, for allowing us to use their beautiful kitchen in Sag Harbor for the cover of our book; to Wittendale's Florist & Greenhouses in East Hampton, for their willingness to supply us on a moment's notice with a spectacular ficus tree for our cover shot; to Lucy Biery, for feeding us pasta during the worst blizzard we've ever encountered; to Nathaniel Bisson and Lief Anne Stiles, our models; and to the Amagansett Eastside Tennis Club. We would also like to thank Albert Stiles for his assistance researching hardware.

As always, thanks to everyone at Chapters Publishing for their support and enthusiasm in all our endeavors: Barry Estabrook, our publisher, Sandy Taylor, our editor, Eugenie Delaney, the book designer, Emily Stetson, our copy editor, Alice Lawrence, the managing editor, and Melissa Cochran, the editorial assistant. A terrific team!

A special thanks to our photographer, Skip Hine, who is able to shoot beautiful photographs in both blizzard and heat-wave conditions.

Contents

Section V
Office & Entertainment Storage

Section VI
Outdoor, Garden & Sports Equipment Storage

Introduction

THERE IS SOMETHING very satisfying about having your house in order: papers filed and files shelved; tools stored or displayed on the wall; clothes arranged neatly and conveniently; sporting equipment out of the way yet within easy reach. An organized environment streamlines your day, eliminating the stress of constantly looking for things, and provides you with more time for pleasurable activities.

Clutter, on the other hand, can create chaos, inefficiency and frustration. But an individual's personal habits aren't always at the root of the problem: Sometimes the culprit is simply a lack of adequate storage space within the home.

Every house and apartment has wasted or underutilized space that can be put to good use. This does not mean stacking box upon box in the attic or shoving outdated clothing farther into the dark recesses of a deep closet. To make the most of the potential storage space in your home, begin by taking an inventory. Examine your living quarters and make a list of the belongings that need more storage space. Categorize them according to whether they are used often, only sporadically or possibly not at all. If they fall into the latter category, consider donating them to a thrift shop or recycling center.

Next, check out all the areas in your home that have wasted space and, based on the inventory you've done, try to determine which areas are appropriate for storing particular possessions. Scanning the projects in this book will help you decide how to solve your specific storage problems.

Adequate storage is especially critical in the kitchen. In order to have a cleared, clutter-free work space, cooking and cleaning utensils need to be out of sight but at the same time easily accessible.

While writing this book, we were forced to examine our own household problems, which included disorganized and inadequate kitchen storage. The first area we dealt with was under the kitchen sink—a dark, damp space filled with random cleaning supplies hiding between pipes and drains. The four easy-to-build, under-the-sink storage projects keep everything hidden from sight when the kitchen cabinet doors are closed yet clearly exposed and readily available when the doors are open. Equally important, the storage units can be easily removed in case the under-sink plumbing needs to be repaired.

With more and more people working at home, the home office has become another area where efficient storage of papers, files and office equipment is essential. We have included several projects that can help you organize your personal work space and integrate it into your home.

In addition to showing you how to turn wasted space into usable storage areas, this book demonstrates how to make hard-to-reach or inconvenient areas in the attic, the basement or the garage more accessible. There are quick-fix storage tips; building projects designed specifically for the bathroom, bedroom, kitchen, home office, entertainment center and family room; and simple solutions for storing sporting goods, outdoor equipment and garden supplies. Each project in Sections IV through VI includes a materials list, plans, detailed illustrations and easy-to-follow instructions. Using readily available materials and basic carpentry skills, you can easily expand the storage space in your home and, as a result, improve the quality of your life.

General Information

Measurements & Materials

Most do-it-yourselfers know that lumber is sold in nominal dimensions, which means that a board such as a 2x4 actually measures only 1½ inches by 3½ inches. This is a result of the final planing, surfacing and anticipated shrinkage of the wood as it dries. This ½-inch discrepancy changes in wide boards, so that lumber with a nominal measurement of 8 inches or more in width measures ¾ inch less. The difference in the thickness of the boards, however, remains the same. So a 2x8, for example, measures 1½ inches by 7¼ inches (not 7½ inches).

Plywood, which is generally sold in 4x8-foot sheets of ⅛-inch, ¼-inch, ½-inch and ¾-inch thicknesses, has fallen victim to the same discrepancy. Bring your tape measure and your reading glasses to the lumberyard when you are picking out plywood, because it can be ¹⁄₃₂ to ¹⁄₁₆ inch less in thickness than what is referred to. Unless this is taken into consideration when building a project, your joints (if cut exactly as specified) will always be a little off. We have made an effort to take these discrepancies into account when we give you the measurements and cutting plans for each project.

Plywood is made up of several thin wood plies, or layers, of wood, glued together. Exterior plywood is made with waterproof glue and is commonly available at lumberyards in face grades of A, B and C.

For indoor projects, look for a grade that has at least one good side, to use for the exposed side of your project. Also, try to avoid sheets with numerous voids or gaps in the edges. When appearance is important, use a cabinet-grade plywood, which is faced with an unblemished veneer of birch, oak, lauan or Baltic, to mention a few of the most commonly available.

For most projects in this book, you won't need plywood in pieces wider than 2 feet. Because a 4x8 sheet of plywood is heavy and awkward to handle, we recommend sawing it in half, lengthwise, before you begin cutting out pieces for your project—provided the measurements permit such a cut, of course. The easiest solution is to have it cut at the lumberyard, but if that's not an option, do it yourself with a portable circular saw as soon as you get it home. If you have to carry a full sheet of ¾-inch plywood by

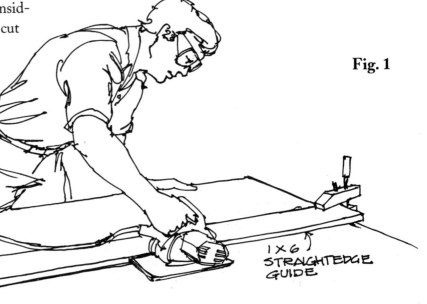

Fig. 1

1 X 6
STRAIGHTEDGE
GUIDE

Fig. 2A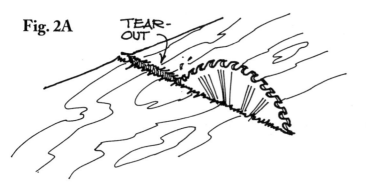

Fig. 2B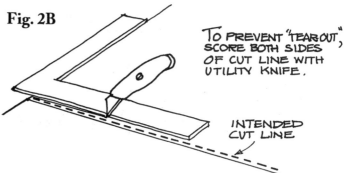

yourself, try to balance it over your shoulder and head with one hand on top and the other turned out, gripping the bottom. Be sure to wear gloves to avoid getting splinters.

To cut a sheet of plywood into two 2x8-foot pieces, lay it on two sawhorses or other supports, and slide two long boards under it so both of the 2-foot-wide pieces will be supported when the cut is finished. Measure and mark where the 24-inch center is on each end and position the saw blade so that it straddles the mark. Use a very straight 1x6 as a guide for the saw, placing it up against the base of your saw and clamping it to the plywood. While cutting the plywood, hold the saw firmly against the 1x6 as you cut along the line (see Fig. 1).

When cutting plywood across the grain, the blade will have a tendency to create "tear-out," surface splintering of the wood plies (see Fig. 2A). To prevent this, score both sides of the cut line with a utility knife (see Fig. 2B).

Tool Tips & Tricks of the Trade

TABLE SAWS

As you look through this book, you'll notice that many of the projects require the use of a table saw. Although we like to keep the amount of tools necessary to a minimum, we have included a table saw, as we feel it is indispensable for the average woodworking shop.

Use this saw with respect. Although extremely useful, a table saw is a powerful tool that operates at

a high speed. Keep the following tips in mind with *every* cut:

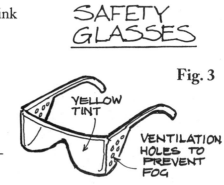

Fig. 3

• Even if you think they look silly, wear plastic safety glasses, especially when making rip cuts. We like the yellow-tinted glasses, which have the added feature of making cloudy days look sunny (see Fig. 3). When cutting cedar or pressure-treated woods, it's also a good idea to wear a dust mask.

• Always use a push stick in order to keep your hands away from the saw blade when feeding pieces of wood through the saw (see Fig. 4). **NOTE:** For viewing purposes, we've left the blade guard off the illustrations in this book. But for safety, *always* use the guard when operating a table saw.

• Don't attempt to cut small pieces of wood that could fall through or get jammed in the saw blade slot.

• When ripping (cutting with the grain), use a "featherboard" accessory (see Sources) to keep the board lightly pressed against the fence. You can make your own featherboard (see Fig. 4) and clamp it to your table saw, or buy one that fits into the ¾-inch-wide slot normally used for a miter gauge. The store-bought featherboard has an added hold-down feature that prevents kickbacks.

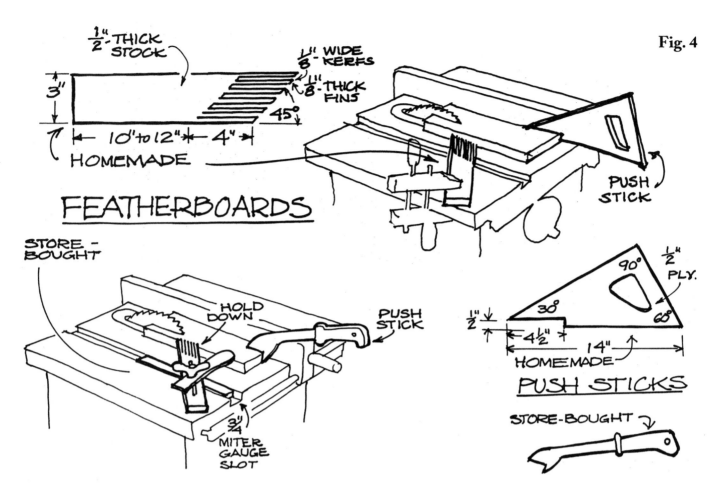

Fig. 4

½"-THICK STOCK

⅛" WIDE KERFS

⅛"-THICK FINS

45°

3"

10" to 12" 4"

HOMEMADE

FEATHERBOARDS

PUSH STICK

STORE-BOUGHT

HOLD DOWN

PUSH STICK

¾"

MITER GAUGE SLOT

½" PLY.

90°

30°

60°

½"

4½"

14"

HOMEMADE

PUSH STICKS

STORE-BOUGHT

David bought his first table saw in 1950 from Sears for $110. Forty-six years later, the same saw (with minor improvements) costs $139 (see Sources). This is about the same price as a good electric jigsaw or a top-of-the-line cordless drill. Not much, when compared with other tools that are used much less frequently. Bench table saws, which sit on top of a work surface, are available through mail-order catalogs for as little as $84.95 and can be shipped directly to you (see Sources).

When you study the cutting plans for our projects, you will notice that occasionally there is an asterisk after a dimension. This means that the material cut away by the saw has been factored into the overall dimension. For example, if a board is to be cut five times, we have allowed for the removal of five ⅛-inch kerf cuts by adding ⅝ inch to the overall dimension.

What is a "kerf cut"? It is the thickness of the cut that is made when a saw passes through the wood.

The sawdust left underneath your work represents the wood that is removed when you make a cut. There is a carpenter's expression, "leave the line," which means to make sure that the kerf of the saw is always on the waste side of the marked cutting line (see Fig. 5). Otherwise, you will end up with a finished piece of wood that is shorter or narrower than it was when you first measured it.

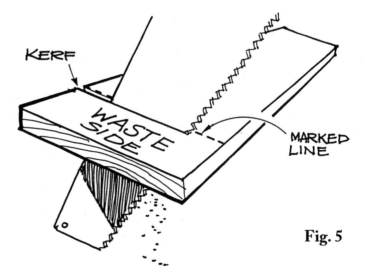

KERF

WASTE SIDE

MARKED LINE

Fig. 5

Fig. 6

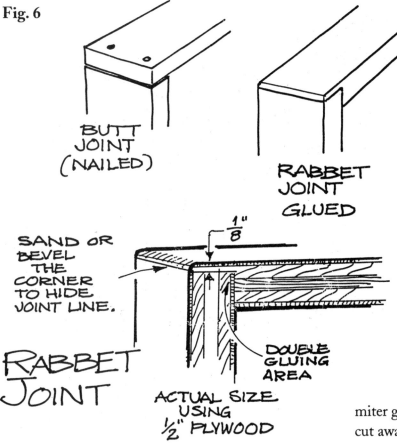

BUTT JOINT (NAILED)

RABBET JOINT GLUED

SAND OR BEVEL THE CORNER TO HIDE JOINT LINE.

$\frac{1}{8}$"

RABBET JOINT

DOUBLE GLUING AREA

ACTUAL SIZE USING $\frac{1}{2}$" PLYWOOD

RABBETS VS. BUTTS

When we built the projects in this book, we used rabbet joints whenever possible. We found that taking the time to include this extra step may actually save time in the assembly, gluing and clamping of the piece, as well as lend strength to the joint. However, because many people may not have the power tools that are required to make rabbet cuts, we have drawn the plans showing simple butt joints that can be made using basic hand tools, which most people have in their home or shop.

If you own a table saw, radial arm saw or table router, we recommend that you revise our dimensions, changing the butt joints to rabbet joints. To do this, look carefully at the plans. In a typical butt joint, one piece of wood is made shorter to accept the thickness of the overlapping piece of wood (see Fig. 6). To change this to a rabbet joint, add the dimension of the thickness of the overlapping wood, minus ⅛ inch, to the length of the shorter piece (see Fig. 6).

Practice making a few rabbet cuts on pieces of scrap wood before you try them on a project. Set up your table saw for cutting rabbet joints by raising the saw blade above the top surface of the table saw. How high you raise it will depend on the thickness of the wood. For ½-inch plywood, for example, you'd raise the blade approximately ⅜ inch, leaving a ⅛-inch lip. Measure and make a mark ½ inch in from the edge of the piece of wood to be rabbeted (see Fig. 7) and place the board on the table saw so the outside edge of the saw blade is just touching the mark (see Fig. 7A). Back the wood off slightly before turning on the saw. Holding the wood snug against the miter gauge, push the wood through the blade. The first cut is the critical one. Remove the wood, pull back the miter gauge and reposition it for another pass. Try to cut away about 3⁄32 inch of wood on each pass, until all the wood in the rabbet groove is removed, leaving you with a lip of about ⅛ inch.

Setting up the saw for a rabbet joint takes only a couple of minutes and not only gives you a much stronger joint with almost twice as much gluing area, but also results in a more professional-looking project. While you have the saw set up, it makes sense to rabbet all the other joints as well.

Fig. 7

$\frac{1}{2}$" OR THICKNESS OF ADJOINING PLYWOOD

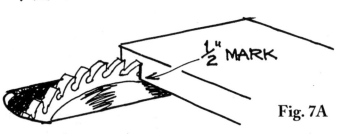

$\frac{1}{2}$" MARK

Fig. 7A

Fig. 8

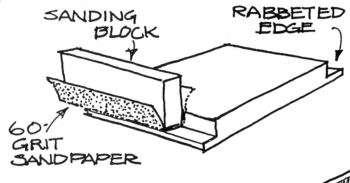

Once the project is completed, slightly round off the corner of the joint, using a sheet of 120-grit sandpaper, followed by 220-grit sandpaper on a block.

You can also use a dado blade, a router or a jointer to make a rabbet joint, but all of these take much longer to set up. Using a table saw will give you a fairly coarse cut as compared to a router cut, but any rough surfaces can be easily smoothed with a file or sandpaper-covered sanding block (see Fig. 8).

Since a rabbet joint is stronger than a butt joint, it is generally not necessary to use nails to hold the pieces together as long as you glue them and clamp them while the glue is drying. This relieves you of the arduous task of countersinking the nails and filling the nail holes with wood putty. You also avoid the risk of hammering a nail out of alignment and having it protrude out the side of the wood, or of having the hammer slip and dent the wood.

GLUING AND CLAMPING

Before gluing and clamping pieces of wood together, always make sure that you have water and a clean rag or sponge nearby. Watch for any glue that drips, seeps out of a joint or runs down the side of the wood, and wipe this up immediately. Glue dries quickly and leaves a stain on wood that often shows up when you are finishing the job. For a rabbet joint, apply the glue in a very thin bead along each surface of the joint and the end grain of the adjoining piece of wood (see Fig. 9). Allow the glue to soak into the end grain for a minute, and if the resulting finish appears dull, apply another very thin coat. Use a small

chip of wood or Popsicle stick with the end cut off square to spread the glue, being careful not to let the glue reach the edge of the wood.

You can use any type of carpenter's glue, but we prefer the water-resistant brands in case the project comes in contact with moisture. Whatever type of glue you use, it should set up rather quickly (15 to 20 minutes), so that you can move on to the next phase of construction. Check all the joints for perfect alignment and be careful not to put any stress on the joints once the glue begins drying. For maximum strength, allow the glue to dry overnight.

For a professional-looking result, always clamp your work together while the glue is drying. A variety of clamps is available (see Fig. 10). For objects 3 to 4 inches in size, we use rubber bands cut from old bicycle inner tubes. For objects 6 to 8 inches in size, we recommend using two wood hand screws, such as Jorgensen's #2 adjustable-style clamps (see also Sources). For larger pieces, over a foot long, we use ½-inch pipe clamps attached to any length of ½-inch black plumber's pipe.

Two other types of useful clamps are spring clamps and the new one-handed clamps, good for clamping objects 9 to 16 inches long.

Fig. 10

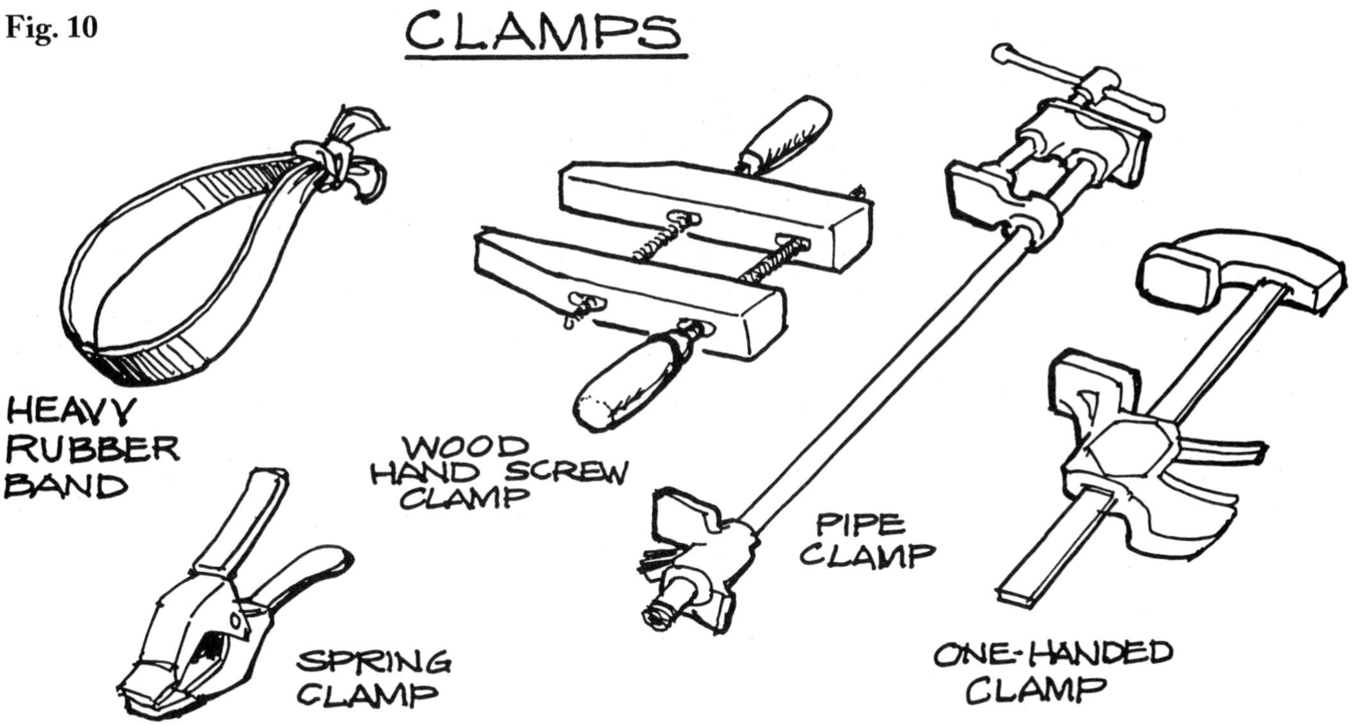

CLAMPS

HEAVY RUBBER BAND

WOOD HAND SCREW CLAMP

SPRING CLAMP

PIPE CLAMP

ONE-HANDED CLAMP

After clamping the pieces together, remember to check all sides to make sure that they are aligned and fit together properly.

Finishing Touches

EDGING

Depending on the kind of plywood you use, you may want to cover up the edges to give the project a more finished look. With a high grade of plywood, such as Baltic, you may choose to leave the edges exposed to show off the plies of wood. On the other hand, the edges of a more economical or less perfect grade of plywood, such as A-C, may contain blemishes, voids and other irregularities. If the plywood is to be stained or painted, you can seal the edges with wood filler, spackle, epoxy or even auto body filler (Bondo), and sand it smooth.

Another alternative is to cover the edges with an edge banding. This is a thin veneer of wood or plastic that comes in a roll and is either self-adhering or heat-sealed to the edge of the plywood.

We prefer to make our own edging and glue it

on, using carpenter's glue. To do this, take a leftover piece of wood from the project you have built and rip-cut it to the same dimension as the plywood edge you are covering. From this piece of wood, rip-cut $\frac{1}{16}$-inch-thick strips (see Fig. 11A), then cut the strips to the appropriate lengths. Apply a bead of carpenter's glue to the back side of each strip and attach it to the plywood edge, using push pins every 3 inches to hold it in place (see Fig. 11B). Once the glue has dried, remove the pins and sand the edges smooth. The holes left by the pins will fill with sawdust and be almost indistinguishable.

SANDING & FINISHING

Although sanding can be one of the most boring parts of woodworking, it is a crucial last step. Nothing creates a more professional, finished look than a perfectly smooth, sanded surface. Sometimes sanding can take almost as long as building the project, but it's worth it, as it makes your woodworking project stand out.

It's generally best to use at least three grades of sandpaper: 60-, 120- and 220-grit. Coarse sandpaper is used more for shaping, while fine sandpaper is for smoothing wood surfaces.

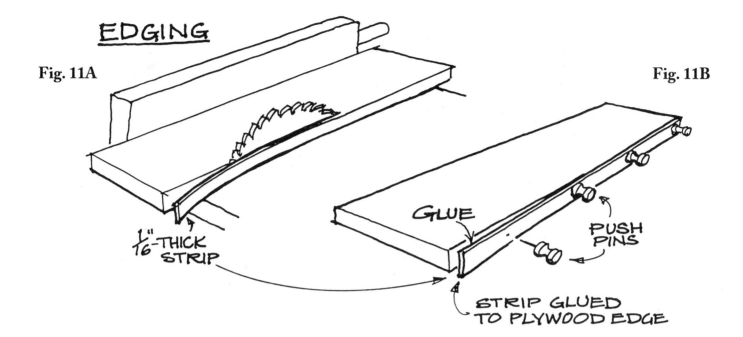

EDGING

Fig. 11A **Fig. 11B**

$\frac{1}{16}$"-THICK STRIP

GLUE

PUSH PINS

STRIP GLUED TO PLYWOOD EDGE

The best—and cheapest—sanding tool is a sanding block made from a scrap piece of 1x4 with a half sheet of sandpaper wrapped around it. Sand all the surfaces until the wood is smooth to the touch, and always sand with the grain of the wood, with the exception of the end grain, which can be sanded in any direction.

For light sanding between coats of varnish, urethane or paint, use 220-grit sandpaper. Cushion the face of the sandpaper by placing a piece of cloth or soft cardboard between the sandpaper and the sanding block.

Attaching to the Wall

SINCE SEVERAL PROJECTS in this book are attached to a wall, it's a good idea to familiarize yourself with the various techniques used for different types of wall materials.

Most houses today are built with ½-inch gypsum wallboard, nailed over 2x4 or 2x6 studs, spaced 16 or 24 inches on-center. Since the wallboard consists of relatively soft plaster sandwiched between two pieces of paper, it has very little holding power, which means nails and screws can easily pull out.

The best way to prevent this from happening is to locate the studs behind the wall and screw through the unit you're hanging, through the wallboard and into the wood studs. To locate wall studs, measure from the nearest corner in 16- or 24-inch increments (depending on the age of your house). If your house was built before 1930, chances are that the studs are 2x4s, spaced 24 inches apart or randomly spaced from the center of one stud to the center of another. Most wall studs built after 1930 are 16 inches on-center, which means the space between the studs is 14½ inches. More recently (after 1970), many builders switched to 2x6 wall studs, spaced 24 inches apart.

Mark where you think the studs are. Then, with the heel of your hand, pound the wall at these locations, listening for the most solid sound. Next, turn off the electricity in that part of your house at the fuse box or circuit breaker, and use a masonry drill to drill a ¼-inch-diameter hole through the wall. Poke a wire coat hanger through the hole to locate the stud (see Fig. 12). Mark where you think the stud is, measure over 16 or 24 inches and make another inspection hole. If you hit wood, you've found the studs. Use a level, held vertically, to draw a light line on the wall where the center of the stud is located.

LOCATING STUDS
CUTAWAY VIEW

Fig. 12

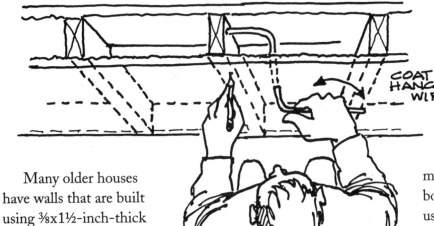

Many older houses have walls that are built using ⅜x1½-inch-thick wood lath, nailed horizontally to the studs. There is a ⅜- to ½-inch-wide space between each strip of lath. The wood lath is then covered with three layers of plaster, ¾ to 1 inch thick. In this instance, you can sometimes get away with using ordinary drywall screws to attach an object to the wall, as long as the screw bites into the wood lath (see Fig. 13). No pilot hole is necessary here. If there is no solid wood behind the wall to screw into, you can use one of the hollow-wall fasteners listed on page 18, available at hardware stores.

EXPANSION BOLTS

Toggle bolts and *molly bolts* are two types of fasteners that expand inside a wall cavity once they are tightened up. Both can be time-consuming to install. The toggle bolt requires a hole big enough to accommodate the two compressed wings of the bolt to be drilled through the plaster, using a masonry bit. (The hole size is indicated on the package.) A smaller hole, the same diameter as the threaded part of the toggle bolt, is drilled through the object to be hung. A washer is attached to the bolt, which is then pushed through the object and into the hole in the wall. The wings spring open against the back side of the wall, inside the wall cavity, after the bolt is tightened with a screwdriver (see Fig. 14).

Molly bolts are similar to toggle bolts in that they are installed in approximately the same fashion and expand once they are on the other side of the wallboard. Be aware that if for some reason you have to remove a molly bolt, the business end of the bolt will fall inside the wall cavity, where it will be impossible to retrieve.

Fig. 13

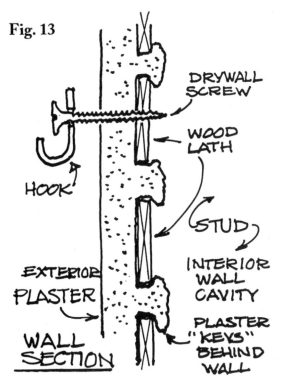

Fig. 14

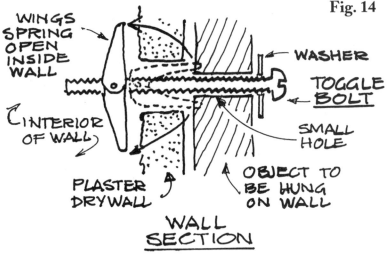

ANCHOR BOLTS

Anchor bolts come in two varieties: plastic and lead (also called lead shields). The former is used with plaster; the latter, with concrete or brick (see Fig. 15). Anchor bolts, like molly and toggle bolts, require a masonry bit (as opposed to a standard drill bit used for metal or wood); however, they are easier to install and to remove than are the other two bolts. The size of the hole required for the anchor is written on the box that it comes in.

Both types of anchors work by expanding into the hole drilled in the plaster or masonry. Begin by drilling the required size hole in the wall and hammering the anchor into the hole. Then screw through the object to be hung and into the hole in the anchor. The screw can be removed and reinserted at any time. The anchor can be removed, or its protruding head can be chiseled off and the hole easily filled with spackle. Or you can recess the anchor with a sharp hammer blow and spackle over it.

Regardless of which fastener you use (we prefer the anchor bolts), be sure to drill a pilot hole first through the object to be attached. Use a nail or a pencil to poke through the hole and mark the wall, then drill the holes for the fasteners.

Below is a list of various-size anchors with their required hole sizes.

Fig. 15

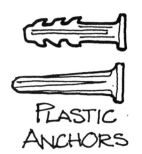

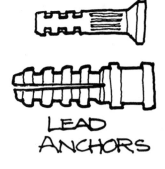

PLASTIC ANCHORS   LEAD ANCHORS

PLASTIC		**LEAD**	
ANCHOR SIZE	BIT SIZE	ANCHOR SIZE	BIT SIZE
#6-8x⅞	³⁄₁₆ inch	⅛x¾ inch	¼ inch
#10-12	¼ inch	³⁄₁₆x1 inch	⁵⁄₁₆ inch
#14-16	⁵⁄₁₆ inch	¼x1 inch	⅜ inch
		¼ inch	½ inch
		⁵⁄₁₆ inch	½ inch
		⅜ inch	⅝ inch
		½ inch	¾ inch

Reclaiming Hard-to-Reach Areas

E VERY HOME has hundreds of cubic feet of potential storage space that goes unused simply because it is hard to reach. Because so much depends on the construction and conditions of your particular house, garage or shed, we are not providing actual plans with dimensions in this section. Instead, we've pointed out a few basic design solutions that should be adaptable to your specific situation.

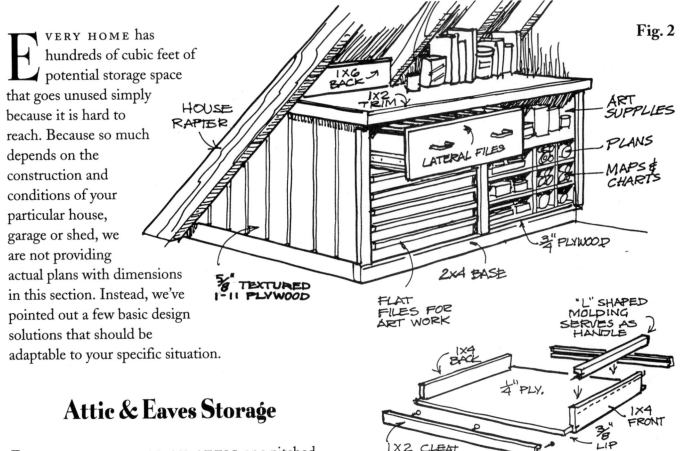

Fig. 2

HOUSE RAFTER

1X6 BACK

1X2 TRIM

LATERAL FILES

ART SUPPLIES

PLANS

MAPS & CHARTS

5/8" TEXTURED 1-11 PLYWOOD

FLAT FILES FOR ART WORK

2X4 BASE

3/4" PLYWOOD

"L" SHAPED MOLDING SERVES AS HANDLE

1X4 BACK

1/4" PLY.

1X4 FRONT

3/8" LIP

1X2 CLEAT WITH 3/8" DADO ATTACHES TO INSIDE WALL OF CABINET.

FLAT FILE DRAWER (NO SIDES) SLIDES ON TWO SIDE CLEATS.

Attic & Eaves Storage

I F YOUR HOUSE HAS AN ATTIC or a pitched roof, you can use the space directly under the eaves to your advantage by building storage cupboards.

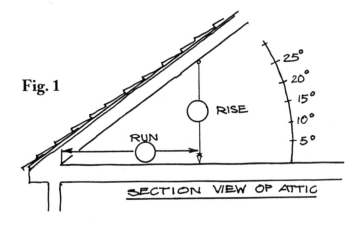

Fig. 1

25°
20°
15°
10°
5°

RISE

RUN

SECTION VIEW OF ATTIC

Find the pitch or slope of your roof by measuring out into the room from where the roof meets the floor and then vertically to the roof. This is called the "run of the rise" (see Fig. 1). Jot down these two measurements and draw them to scale on graph paper. Lay a protractor over your drawing to find the degree of pitch, and use this number to calculate and draw the plans for your storage cupboards. Our eaves storage area is shown in Fig. 2.

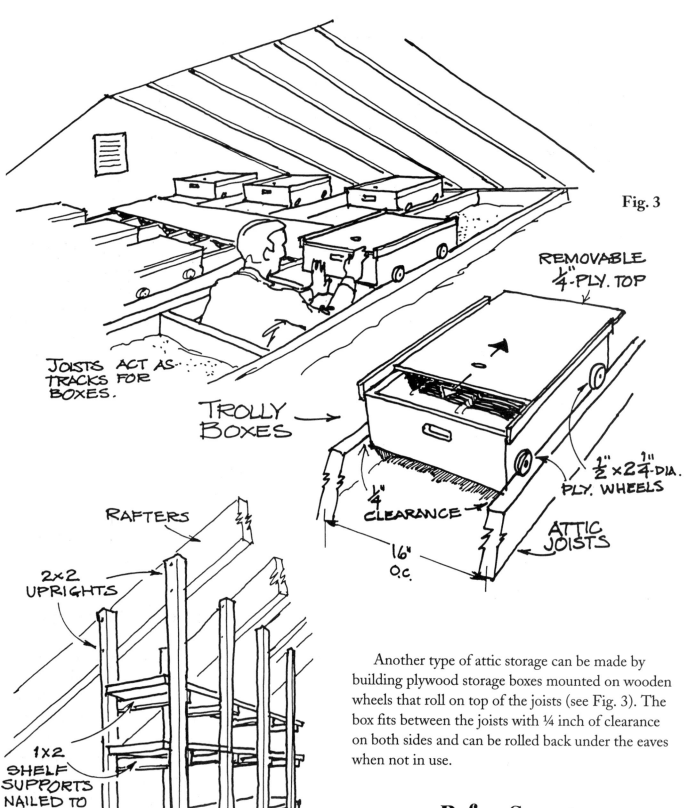

Fig. 3

JOISTS ACT AS TRACKS FOR BOXES.

TROLLY BOXES →

REMOVABLE ¼"-PLY. TOP

¼" CLEARANCE

16" O.C.

$\frac{1}{2}" \times 2\frac{1}{4}"$-DIA. PLY. WHEELS

ATTIC JOISTS

RAFTERS

2×2 UPRIGHTS

1×2 SHELF SUPPORTS NAILED TO UPRIGHTS

RAFTER STORAGE SHELVES

Fig. 4

Another type of attic storage can be made by building plywood storage boxes mounted on wooden wheels that roll on top of the joists (see Fig. 3). The box fits between the joists with ¼ inch of clearance on both sides and can be rolled back under the eaves when not in use.

Rafter Storage

LADDER RACKS ARE USEFUL for either attic or basement storage (see Fig. 4). They can be easily built by cutting and installing 2x2 uprights, connected with 1x2 crosspieces. Screw them to every

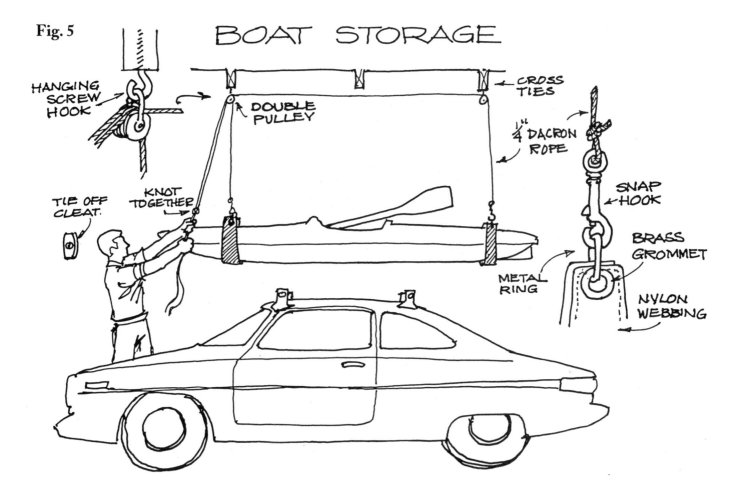

Fig. 5

BOAT STORAGE

HANGING SCREW HOOK

DOUBLE PULLEY

CROSS TIES

¼ DACRON ROPE

TIE OFF CLEAT.

KNOT TOGETHER

SNAP HOOK

BRASS GROMMET

METAL RING

NYLON WEBBING

rafter or joist, depending on where they are being installed. The distance between the front and back uprights is determined by the width of the boards you are using for shelving. Ladder racks are especially well suited for damp basements, as they keep your valuables above ground level.

Overhead Boat Storage

IF YOU OWN A CANOE, kayak or other small boat and want to store it indoors, you can rig a pulley system that will lift the boat right off your car or trailer and hoist it up to the ceiling of your garage. Use heavy-duty screw hooks to attach to the ceiling joists or rafters and two pulleys: one single and the other double. Depending on the size and weight of your boat (it shouldn't be more than 300 pounds for this storage situation), thread ¼- to ⅜-inch-diameter rope through the pulleys and tie the rope to two snap hooks. Install brass grommets in both ends of two

pieces of 2-inch nylon webbing that are long enough to go around the boat (see Fig. 5), and attach this to metal rings that connect to the snap hooks.

Niches or In-Wall Storage

THE AVERAGE HOUSE has approximately 2,000 square feet of storage space that is never used, much of it behind the interior walls, between the wall studs. If the storage space you need is 14½ inches wide or less, you can build a niche between two wall studs. A wall niche is perfect for toiletries or cosmetics in the bathroom, spices in the kitchen, decorative items in the living room or auto supplies in the garage. We built Jeanie's mother a bathroom niche to hold a first-aid box.

The first step is to locate the studs behind the walls (see page 16, Attaching to the Wall). Once you've located the wall studs, run a heavy-duty,

Fig. 6

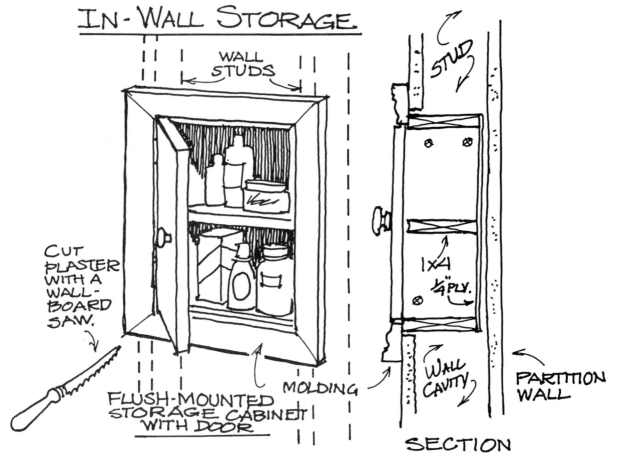

IN·WALL STORAGE.

WALL STUDS

CUT PLASTER WITH A WALL-BOARD SAW.

FLUSH-MOUNTED STORAGE CABINET WITH DOOR

MOLDING

STUD

1×4
¼" PLY.

WALL CAVITY

PARTITION WALL

SECTION

IN·WALL BOOKCASE

1×6

2"

IN·WALL STORAGE STANDS 2" OUT FROM WALL.

Fig. 7

three-prong, grounded extension cord to your work area. After you have determined where the niche should go, use a framing square to mark the outside dimensions on your wall.

Next, make a box frame to fit in the hole you have made. Decide whether you want the box to be flush with the

wall (see Fig. 6) or to stand out from it (see Fig. 7). If it is to be flush, use 1x4 lumber; if it is to protrude out from the wall, use 1x6 lumber. Glue and nail the four frame pieces together and add shelves that are spaced appropriately for the items you will be storing. Cut, glue and nail a ¼-inch birch plywood back to the frame, with the good side facing inside the cabinet.

Under-Counter Corner Storage

EVERY KITCHEN DESIGNER is faced with the problem of how to use the corner space underneath a kitchen counter. You can, of course, buy a plastic "lazy Susan," sold in most houseware stores, which makes use of part of the space and offers limited access. Another, more functional, solution is to make this space accessible to an adjacent room by removing the wall on the back side of the corner space.

Fig. 8

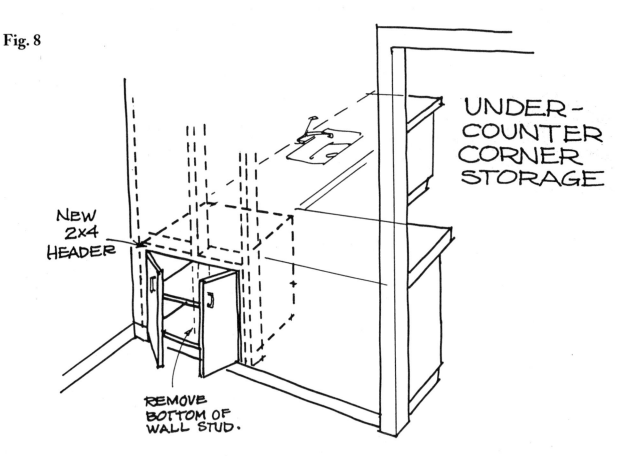

NEW 2x4 HEADER

UNDER- COUNTER CORNER STORAGE

REMOVE BOTTOM OF WALL STUD.

To remove the wall section, measure and mark the size of the opening you prefer, then carefully cut it out, using a reciprocating saw. If you cut through more than one stud, you will need to support the center stud with a horizontal header (see Fig. 8), then build a box as described earlier.

David's brother put his corner storage space to good use by turning it into a wine storage area, accessed by the dining room. Other ideas are for storing firewood, stashing foul-weather gear like galoshes or winter boots or even stockpiling pet food, depending upon what room the space opens into.

Simple Storage Solutions

ITH A LITTLE INGENUITY, you can come up with all kinds of storage solutions to fit your specific needs. Here are a few examples of what we've done.

Lawn Chair Storage

LAWN CHAIRS can be hung in a shed, garage or basement by drilling ⅝-inch-diameter holes in two 2x4 studs and inserting ⅝-inch-diameter dowels at a 15-degree angle (see Fig. 1). If you are storing the chairs in a basement with masonry or stone walls, you can create your own "wall studs" by attaching two 2x4s to the wall with lag screws and lead anchors.

Bicycle Storage

IF YOU DON'T HAVE TIME to build the floor-mounted bicycle rack described in this book (see page 136), an alternative is to store your bikes by suspending them from the ceiling in your garage, shed or basement. To do this, take two wire coat hangers and twist them to form two hooks (see Fig. 2). Tie a ³⁄₁₆-inch-diameter rope to each hook and thread the other ends of the ropes through two small pulleys attached to the ceiling joists by heavy-duty screw hooks. The free end of the rope is pulled to raise the bicycle and is tied off at a cleat mounted to the wall.

Fig. 2

Fig. 1

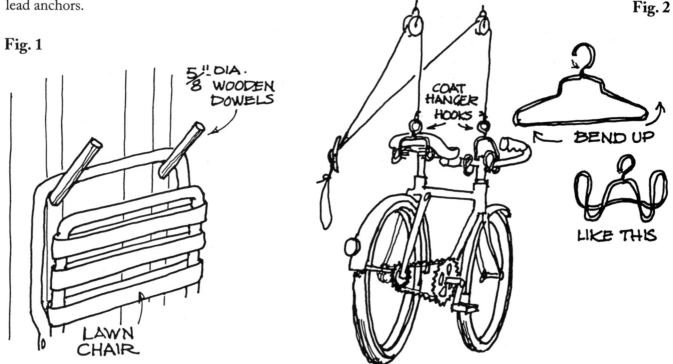

⅝" DIA. WOODEN DOWELS

LAWN CHAIR

COAT HANGER HOOKS

BEND UP

LIKE THIS

Foot-Activated Drawer

EVERYONE NEEDS A PLACE to keep miscellaneous odds and ends. Often these items end up in a box, shoved underneath a work space in a difficult-to-reach area. To facilitate retrieving these items, attach a wire pull or wooden handle to the front of the box and set it on top of a ¾-inch-diameter wooden dowel. Use the handle on the box to lift and pull out the box with the toe of your foot. You'll be surprised how easy this is, and it eliminates the possibility of straining your back when pulling in a bent-over position (see Fig. 3).

Fig. 3

LOOSE WOOD DOWEL

Wall-Stud-Support Shelves

IF THE WALL STUDS in your garage or shed are exposed, you can use the studs as supports for shelving. Notch out a 2x6 board to fit around the studs and then screw it to the studs (see Fig. 4).

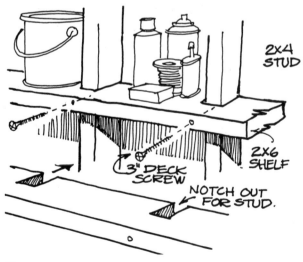

2x4 STUD

2x6 SHELF

3" DECK SCREW

NOTCH OUT FOR STUD.

Fig. 4

Open Shelves

MOST HOMEOWNERS or apartment dwellers are faced with the problem of storing past tax returns, receipts for paid bills, legal files and other miscellaneous papers. A simple solution is to build open storage shelves from two 4x8 sheets of ¾-inch plywood and one 4x8 sheet of ¼-inch plywood. Cut the ¾-inch plywood into the dimensions shown (see Fig. 5). Nail the ¼-inch plywood for the back to the sides and then nail shelves between the sides. To stiffen the 4-foot span, nail a 1x2 strip 46 inches long to the front edge of each shelf. Also, nail through the back piece into the back of each shelf.

Fig. 5

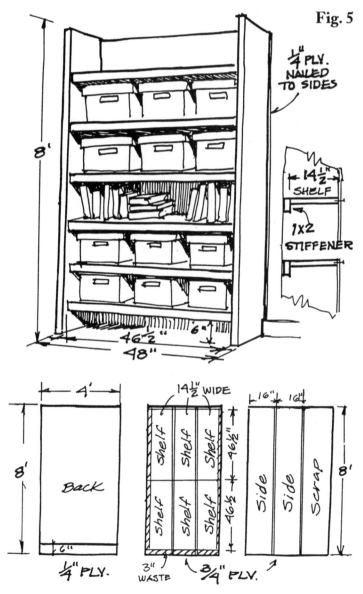

¼" PLY. NAILED TO SIDES

14½" SHELF

1x2 STIFFENER

8'

46½"

6"

48"

4'

8'

Back

¼" PLY.

14½" WIDE

Shelf · Shelf · Shelf

Shelf · Shelf · Shelf

46½"

3" WASTE

¾" PLY.

16" · 16"

Side · Side · Scrap

8'

Fig. 6

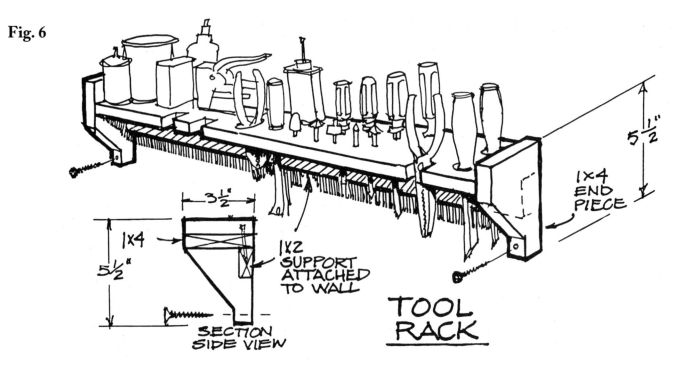

SECTION SIDE VIEW

1x4

3½"

5½"

1x2 SUPPORT ATTACHED TO WALL

TOOL RACK

5½"

1x4 END PIECE

Hand-Tool Rack

Every workshop needs racks for tools and shelves for storage. The tool rack shown here (see Fig. 6) is easy to make since it only requires 1x4 and 1x2 lumber. The 1x2 is used as a support for the shelf and a means for screwing the shelf to the wall. You'll need to cut the two pieces of 1x4 for the ends, then lay out your hand tools and draw on the remaining 1x4 where you need to drill holes or make notches to accommodate the various tools. Nail the 1x4 end pieces to the 1x4 shelf top, allowing a ½-inch lip above the ends of the shelf to prevent items from falling off. Screw the 1x2 support piece to the wall and nail the shelf top to the 1x2 support. Then screw the end pieces into the wall.

Lightweight Work Surface

Sometimes you need extra work space for occasional chores such as potting plants, mixing paint or fixing an electric lamp. The work surface/storage shelf illustrated here (see Fig. 7) is lightweight and uses readily available materials. Cut the ends of the 1x2 bracket pieces at a 45-degree angle and nail them together. Attach one bracket to the wall every 32 inches, using ¼x3-inch lag screws (bolts). Nail the two 1x8 top boards to the brackets, and trim the front edge with a piece of 1x2.

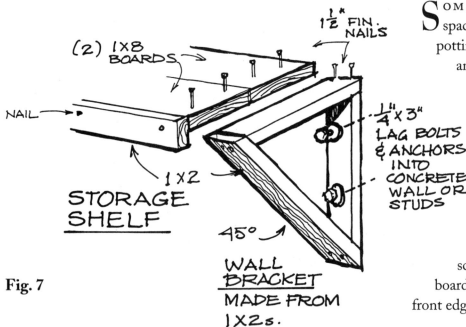

(2) 1X8 BOARDS

1½" FIN. NAILS

NAIL

1X2

STORAGE SHELF

¼" x 3" LAG BOLTS & ANCHORS INTO CONCRETE WALL OR STUDS

45°

WALL BRACKET MADE FROM 1X2s.

Fig. 7

Bedroom, Bath & Kitchen Storage

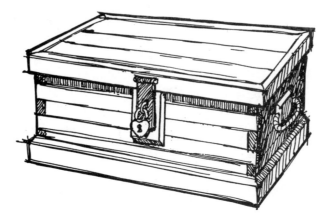

Under-Bed Storage Box on Rollers

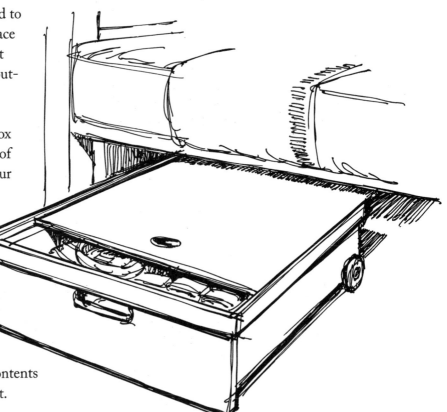

THIS STORAGE BOX is designed to fit under most beds, utilizing space that is usually wasted. It rolls out easily and is a convenient way to hold out-of-season clothes or linens. Made from plywood of two different thicknesses (¼ inch and ½ inch), the 24x24-inch box uses only one-quarter of a sheet or less of each. This makes it possible to build four under-bed storage boxes from two 4x8 sheets of plywood, with very little waste. The box rolls on two back wheels cut out of scrap ½-inch plywood, using a 2⅛-inch hole saw. The front face extends below the bottom to keep the box level and prevent it from rolling around. A removable lid slides over the top, ensuring that the contents of the box remain clean and free of dust.

MATERIALS LIST (FOR ONE BOX)

Quantity	Size	Description	Location or Use
1	24x24 inches	½-inch bass plywood	front, back & sides
1	24x24 inches	¼-inch birch plywood	top panel
1	23½x24 inches	¼-inch birch plywood	bottom
1	24 inches	⅜ x ⅜-inch #2 pine	cleat
1	72¾ inches	¼ x 1½-inch clear lattice	top lip
1 box	1½-inch	finish nails	
1 box	1-inch	wire nails	
2	1¼-inch	#10 roundhead screws with washers	
1 bottle	8 ounces	carpenter's glue	
1 sheet	120-grit	sandpaper	
1 sheet	220-grit	sandpaper	
1 can	10 ounces	water-based wood putty	
1 pint		clear waterborne acrylic urethane wood finish	

Fig. 1

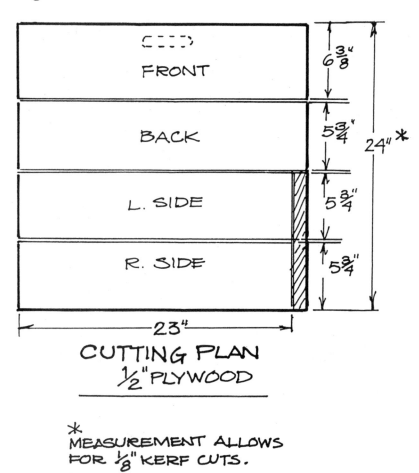

FRONT

6 3/8"

BACK

5 3/4"

24" *

L. SIDE

5 3/4"

R. SIDE

5 3/4"

23"

CUTTING PLAN
1/2" PLYWOOD

*
MEASUREMENT ALLOWS
FOR 1/8" KERF CUTS.

Referring to the Cutting Plan (see Fig. 1), cut out the sides, the front and the back pieces from the sheet of ½-inch plywood. Sand these pieces on what will be the inside face of the box, using 120- and 220-grit sandpaper, mounted on an electric palm sander.

To assemble the box, first set up a solid back stop by temporarily screwing a scrap 2x4 to your work surface (see Fig. 2). Arrange the front, back and side pieces so they are upside down, with the extending edge of the front piece facing up, and the front and back pieces overlapping the sides. Start three 1½-inch finish nails at each end of the front piece. Apply a bead of glue to the back side of the front piece where it meets the sides, and carefully nail the front to the sides (see Fig. 2). Turn the box around and repeat the process for the back piece. Check to make sure that the four pieces are square with one another. Allow about 20 minutes for the glue to set.

While you are waiting, cut out the 24x24-inch top and the 23½x24-inch bottom pieces from the sheet of ¼-inch plywood (see Fig. 3). Sand all the surfaces and edges, using 120- and 220-grit sandpaper. Glue and nail the 23½x24-inch bottom piece to

Fig. 2

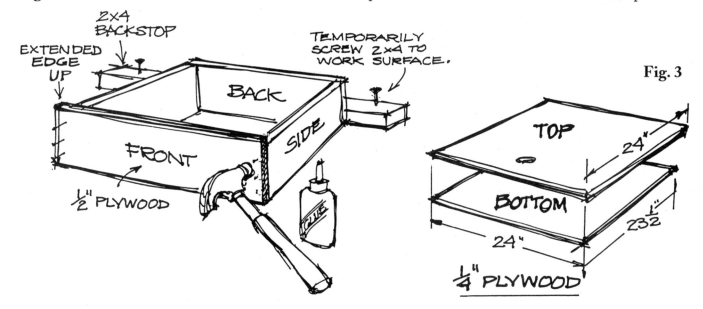

2x4 BACKSTOP

EXTENDED EDGE UP

TEMPORARILY SCREW 2x4 TO WORK SURFACE.

BACK

SIDE

FRONT

1/2" PLYWOOD

Fig. 3

TOP

24"

BOTTOM

24"

23 1/2"

1/4" PLYWOOD

Fig. 4

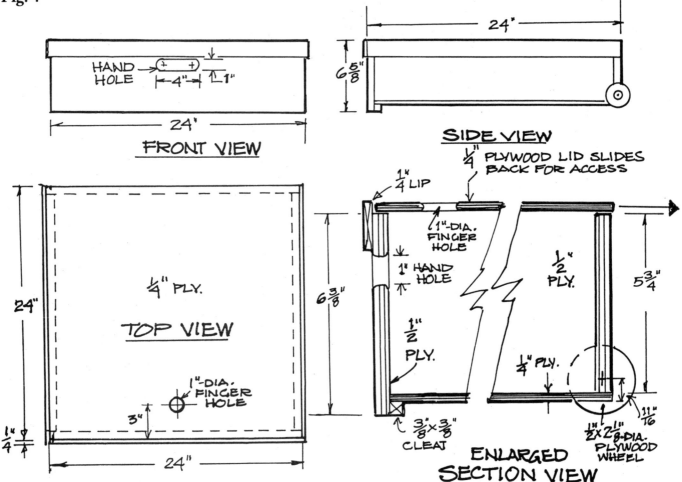

the bottom of the box, using 1-inch wire nails spaced every 3 inches along the sides and the back.

To support the front edge of the ¼-inch plywood bottom, cut, glue and clamp a 24-inch-long cleat made from the ⅜x⅜-inch pine to the underneath inside edge (see Fig. 4, Enlarged Section View).

Cut two pieces of ¼x1½-inch clear lattice, each 24 inches long, and glue them to the sides of the box so that there is a ¼-inch lip protruding above the top of the box's sides (see Fig. 5). Clamp the lattice to the sides. **NOTE:** Place a scrap piece of wood between the clamp and the sides to keep the clamps from denting the lattice as well as to help distribute the pressure of the clamp. When the glue has dried, cut another piece of lattice 24½ inches long and glue it across the top of the front piece, overlapping

the ends of the two lattice pieces on the sides (see Fig. 5).

To make the front hand hole, measure down ⅝ inch below the bottom edge of the front lattice piece and make a mark 1½ inches to either side of the center of the front piece. Using a spade bit, begin a 1-inch-diameter hole at both marks (see Fig. 5), drilling only halfway through the plywood. Turn the front piece over and finish drilling the hole. This is done to avoid "tear-out," or splitting the plywood when the drill exits the hole. Connect the two circles by drawing two parallel lines and creating the elongated shape shown in Fig. 5. Using an electric jigsaw with a fine-toothed (scroll) blade, cut out the hand hole. Round off and smooth the edges, using 120- and 220-grit sandpaper rolled into a tube shape.

Storage Projects You Can Build

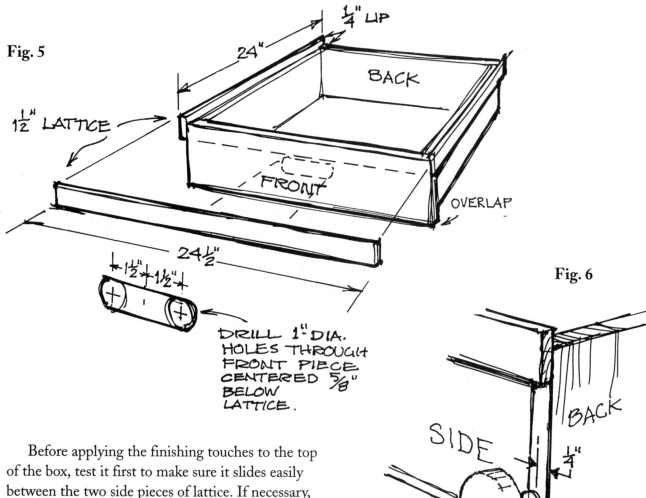

Fig. 5

24"

1/4" UP

BACK

1 1/2" LATTICE

FRONT

OVERLAP

24 1/2"

1 1/2" 1 1/2"

Fig. 6

DRILL 1" DIA. HOLES THROUGH FRONT PIECE CENTERED 5/8" BELOW LATTICE.

SIDE

BACK

1/4"

11/16"

2 1/8"-DIA. PLYWOOD WHEEL

℄

Before applying the finishing touches to the top of the box, test it first to make sure it slides easily between the two side pieces of lattice. If necessary, lightly sand or plane down the edges of the top panel so that it moves back and forth smoothly.

Cut a 1-inch-diameter finger hole, centered 2 inches back from the front edge of the top panel. Using a spade bit, drill the finger hole, using the same technique as you did for the hand hole.

Cut the two wheels from a scrap piece of 1/2-inch plywood, using a 2 1/8-inch hole saw (an essential tool to have if you ever have to install a lockset in a door). The hole saw will create a center hole for each wheel.

Fill any nail holes with wood putty and sand the outside surfaces of the box and wheels with 120- and

220-grit sandpaper, then finish with three coats of a clear waterborne acrylic urethane.

Drill a pilot hole for each wheel in the end grain of the back piece (see Fig. 6), positioning the hole 11/16 inch up from the bottom and 1/4 inch in from the back edge. Screw each wheel into its hole, using a 1 1/4-inch #10 roundhead screw and two washers.

Heirloom Chest

THIS ATTRACTIVE, sturdy, well-constructed chest can be placed at the foot of your bed and used to store blankets, or it can serve as a coffee table in your living room. It can be built out of common ⁵⁄₄ spruce or a more exotic material, such as redwood. Shop around for just the right size and style of hardware to complement its design and show off your workmanship. Early American or Mexican hand-forged pieces (see Sources) are two good suggestions.

Before cutting, begin by sanding the surfaces of the boards that will face inside the chest, using 60-, 120- and 220-grit sandpaper. Because you'll be storing sheets and soft blankets inside the chest and reaching in to remove or replace them, you'll want to sand the wood until it's smooth to the touch.

MATERIALS LIST

Quantity	Size	Description	Location or Use
3	8 feet	⁵⁄₄x8 spruce decking	back, sides & front
1	10 feet	⁵⁄₄x8 spruce decking	top
1	30 inches	⁵⁄₄x8 spruce decking	batten & handle blocks
1	17¼x35½ inches	½-inch A-C plywood	floor
2	10 feet	1x4 #2 pine	top & bottom trim
1	20 inches	1x4 #2 pine	hinge blocks
1 box	2½-inch	galvanized finish nails	
1 box	3½-inch	#8 drywall screws	
1 box	1½-inch	#10 flathead screws	battens, handles
1 bottle	8 ounces	carpenter's glue	
1 can	10 ounces	water-based wood putty	
1 pair	4-inch	"T" hinges with screws	back hinges
1	6-inch	hasp	front latch
1 sheet	60-grit	sandpaper	
1 sheet	120-grit	sandpaper	
1 sheet	220-grit	sandpaper	
1	24 inches	½-inch-dia. rope	handles

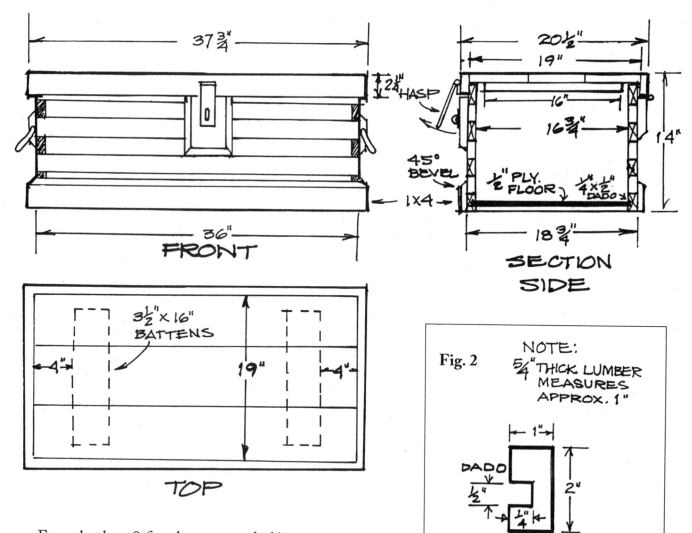

FRONT

TOP

3½" X 16" BATTENS

4" 19" 4"

37¾"

36"

2¼" HASP

1X4

SECTION SIDE

20½"

19"

16"

16¾"

14"

18¾"

45° BEVEL

½" PLY. FLOOR

¼"x1" DADO

Fig. 2

NOTE: 5/4" THICK LUMBER MEASURES APPROX. 1"

DADO ½"

1"

2"

¼"

MAKE A ¼"X ½" DADO TO SUPPORT THE FLOOR IN THE FIRST PIECES.

From the three 8-foot-long spruce decking boards, rip-cut 28 pieces, each measuring 1x2 inches, for the front, back and sides of the chest. Since all the strips must have absolutely square edges, cut ¼ inch off the rounded edge of each 5/4x8 board before ripping it into three 2-inch-wide strips (see Fig. 1).

Fig. 1

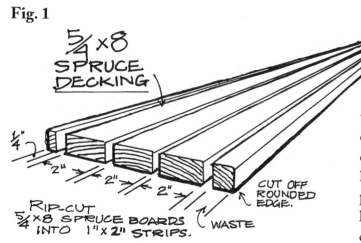

5/4 x8 SPRUCE DECKING

¼"

2" 2" 2"

RIP-CUT 5/4 x 8 SPRUCE BOARDS INTO 1"x 2" STRIPS.

WASTE

CUT OFF ROUNDED EDGE.

Cut eight of the strips 36 inches long, six 34 inches long, eight more 16¾ inches long, and six more 18¾ inches long. The front and back of the chest is constructed by alternating 36-inch and 34-inch strips of wood; the sides, by alternating the 16¾-inch and 18¾-inch strips.

Select two 36-inch-long strips, one each for the front and back, and two 16¾-inch strips, one for each side. Referring to Fig. 2, make a ½-inch-wide dado, ¼ inch deep, in these four strips of wood to hold the floor of the chest. Cut a piece of ½-inch plywood for the floor, 17¼ by 35½ inches, and fit it loosely into the dadoes. After the floor is placed securely into the grooves, nail the bottom strips of the

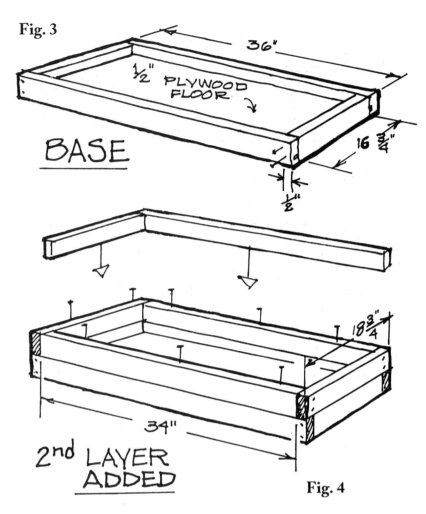

Fig. 3

36"

½" PLYWOOD FLOOR

16 ¾"

½"

BASE

18 ¾"

34"

2nd LAYER ADDED

Fig. 4

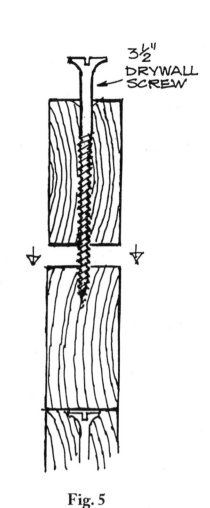

3½" DRYWALL SCREW

Fig. 5

chest together, hammering two 2½-inch finish nails ½ inch from the ends of the front and back strips and into the ends of the side strips (see Fig. 3).

Position another layer of the 1x2-inch strips of wood over the first layer, alternating the corner joints, log cabin style. Nail the ends as described above, then glue them to the first layer (see Fig. 4). For added strength, use 3½-inch drywall screws to attach the second layer to the first layer (see Fig. 5). Make sure the heads of the screws are countersunk (screwed below the surface of the wood). Continue gluing and screwing the strips of wood until the chest reaches a height of 14 inches (seven "tiers").

Set the nail heads, fill the holes with wood putty and sand the outside of the chest, using 60-, 120- and 220-grit sandpaper.

Cut the remaining 10-foot-long ⁵⁄₄x8 board into three equal pieces for the chest top (see Fig. 6). Glue and clamp them together, allowing them to dry overnight. Then cut the panel so it measures 19 inches wide. **NOTE:** Before you do this, check to make sure the top of the chest overlaps the base by ⅛ inch on all sides. Cut the length of the top to 36¼ inches.

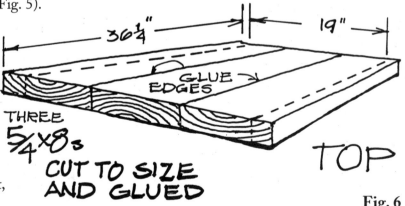

36¼"

19"

GLUE EDGES

THREE ⁵⁄₄x8s CUT TO SIZE AND GLUED

TOP

Fig. 6

Fig. 7

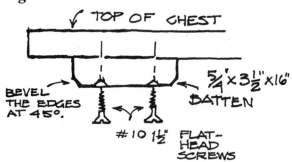

Fig. 8

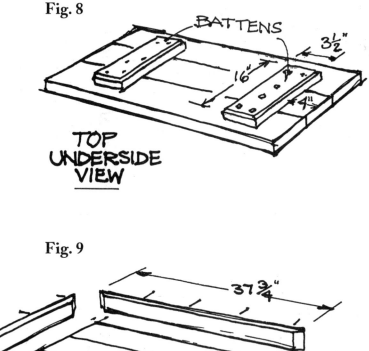

To strengthen the top, cut the 30-inch ⁵⁄₄x8 into a 16-inch-long section, then rip-cut it into two battens, each 3½ inches wide. Sand or bevel the edges on one side of each batten (see Fig. 7). Then, placing the battens parallel and 4 inches in from each end of the top, attach them to the underneath side of the top, using glue and 1½-inch #10 flathead screws (see Fig. 8).

Fig. 9

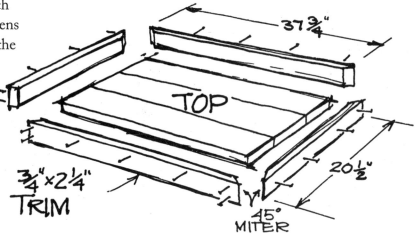

To give the chest a classical look, use #2 pine to trim the top. From a 10-foot-long 1x4, rip-cut a 2¼-inch-wide strip, then cut two 37¾-inch-long pieces and two 20½-inch-long pieces. Miter the ends at a 45-degree angle and glue and nail them to the outside edges of the top, using 2½-inch finish nails spaced 4 inches apart (see Fig. 9).

Trim the bottom of the chest with base molding by cutting the remaining 10-foot-long 1x4 into two 37½-inch-long pieces and two 20¼-inch-long pieces. Miter the ends 45 degrees and use a table saw to bevel the top edges at a 45-degree angle. Glue and nail these trim pieces to the bottom of the chest (see Fig. 10). Set the nail heads, fill the holes with wood putty and sand the wood smooth.

To make hinge blocks for the top, cut two 6-inch-long pieces of 1x4 (see Fig. 11). Bevel all except the top edges to a 45-degree angle. Glue and screw each hinge block to the top of the back of the chest, 4 inches from each back side edge (see Fig. 12).

Fig. 10

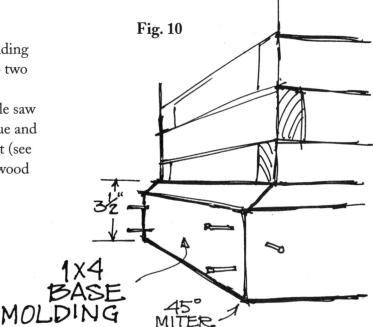

Fig. 11

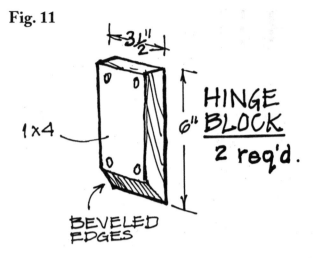

HINGE BLOCK
2 req'd.

1x4

6"

3½"

BEVELED EDGES

Fig. 12

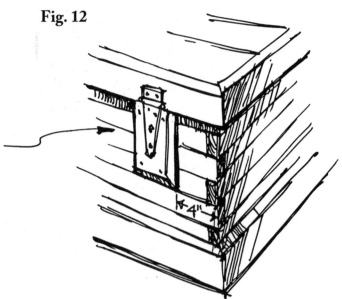

4"

HASP

EYE PAD

Fig. 13

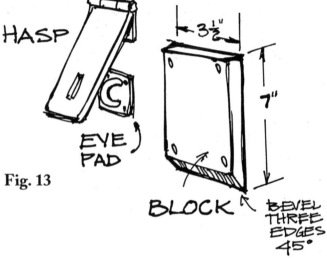

3½"

7"

BLOCK

BEVEL THREE EDGES 45°

½x½-inch dado across the middle of the back sides (see Fig. 14). Cut the ½-inch-diameter rope into two equal pieces and squeeze the rope ends into the dado. Screw each block onto the center of each side of the trunk, 3 inches down from the top edge. To hold the ropes in place, screw two 1½-inch #10 flat-head screws through the block and into the body of the rope (see Fig. 14).

This chest can be finished in many ways—by staining, "antiquing" or simply waxing the wood. We wanted ours to look as though it had had some rough handling, so we "antiqued" it by beating it with a chain, jabbing it with an ice pick and round-ing off the corners.

Screw two 4-inch "T" hinges to the top trim and the 3½x6-inch hinge blocks (see Fig. 12).

You also need to make a small wooden block for the hasp to attach to. From the remaining piece of 1x4, cut a block 3½ inches by 7 inches long. Bevel all but the top edge to a 45-degree angle (see Fig. 13). Glue and screw this block to the top middle of the front of the chest. Screw the top of the hasp to the top trim and screw the eye pad to the 3½x7-inch hasp block, making sure that the two pieces will interlock correctly.

For the handles, cut two 6½x4-inch pieces of ⁵⁄₄x8 spruce and bevel all four edges. Cut a

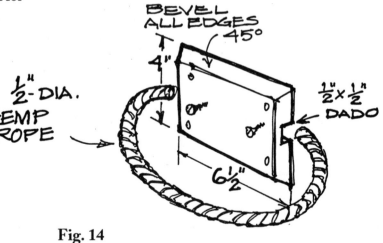

BEVEL ALL EDGES 45°

4"

½"-DIA. HEMP ROPE

½" x ½" DADO

6½"

Fig. 14

Toilet Paper Holder

THIS EASY-TO-MAKE holder can be constructed in less than an hour. We made ours out of rough cedar to match the bathroom wall and applied a milky white stain. The top of the dispenser protects the toilet paper from shower sprays, sink spills and the antics of curious cats inclined to unroll the paper with their claws. The design also makes it easy to remove and insert rolls of toilet paper.

With the Cutting Plan as your guide (see Fig. 1), use a hand saw or a table saw to cut out the sides and top pieces from the 1x8 board. Make a mark in the center of each side piece, then drill a 1¼-inch-diameter hole at these center points (see Fig. 2). **TIP:** To avoid tear-out, start the hole on one side of the wood and when the point of the drill shows through the other side,

remove the drill, turn the board over and complete the hole by drilling through the second side.

Glue the two side pieces to the 7x9⅞-inch ¼-inch plywood back piece (see Fig. 3). Once the glue has dried, nail the back to the side pieces, using 1-inch galvanized wire nails.

Bevel the top back edge of the top piece at a 30-degree angle, then glue and nail it to the side pieces, using 1½-inch galvanized finish nails (see Fig. 4).

Measure in ⅝ inch from each end of the 8½-inch length of 1⅛-inch-diameter dowel and cut a ⅛-inch-deep, 1-inch-wide recessed shoulder. Do this by holding one end of the dowel against the miter gauge of the table saw and rolling the dowel

---

MATERIALS LIST

Quantity	Size	Description	Location or Use
1	26 inches	1x8 pine or cedar	sides, top
1	7x9⅞ inches	¼-inch plywood	back
1	8½ inches	1⅛-inch-diameter wood dowel	
1 handful	1-inch	galvanized wire nails	back & side pieces
1 handful	1½-inch	galvanized finish nails	top edge
1 bottle	8 ounces	carpenter's glue	
2	1½-inch	#8 brass roundhead screws	back
1 pint		Olympic White stain or paint of choice	

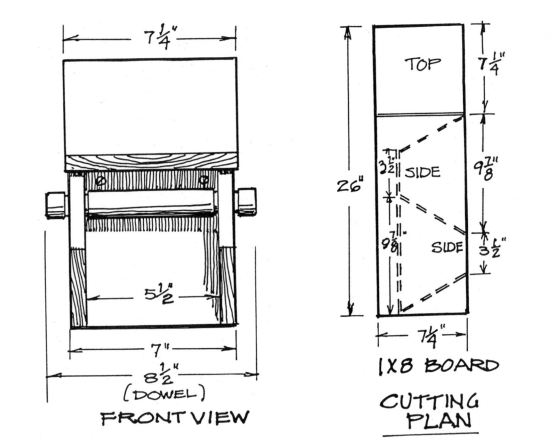

7¼"

TOP

7¼"

26"

3½" SIDE 9⅞"

SIDE

9⅞" 3½"

7¼"

I X 8 BOARD

CUTTING
PLAN

7"

¼
PLY.
BACK

9⅞"

Fig. 1

FRONT VIEW

7¼"

5½"

7"

8½"
(DOWEL)

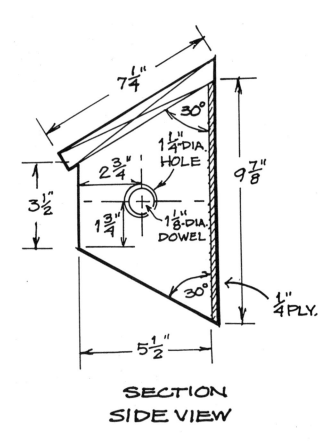

7¼"

30°

1¼"-DIA.
HOLE

2¾"

9⅞"

3½"

1¾"

1⅛"-DIA.
DOWEL

30°

¼ PLY.

5½"

SECTION
SIDE VIEW

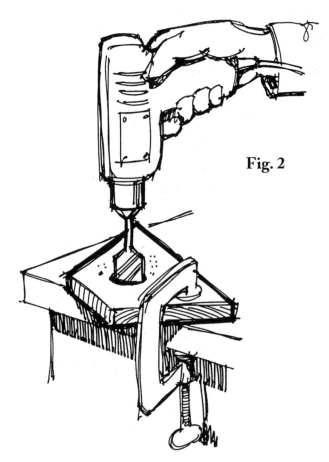

Fig. 2

Storage Projects You Can Build

Fig. 3

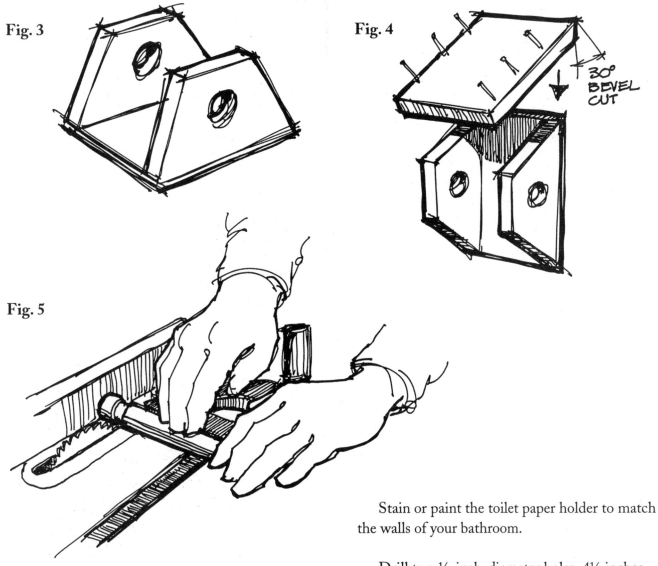

Fig. 4

30°
BEVEL
CUT

Fig. 5

over the blade, which is set ⅛ inch above the surface of the table saw (see Fig. 5). Test-fit the dowel in the two side holes to make sure that it turns smoothly.

Stain or paint the toilet paper holder to match the walls of your bathroom.

Drill two ⅛-inch-diameter holes, 4¼ inches apart, in the plywood back piece and attach the unit to the bathroom wall with two 1½-inch brass screws (see page 16, Attaching to the Wall).

Toothbrush & Cup Holder

WHETHER YOUR BATHROOM is traditional or contemporary in design, this handy shelf will fit right in and eliminate the clutter that can result from having an assortment of toothbrushes, water glasses and toothpaste tubes covering the countertop. The toothbrush shelf attaches to the wall and accommodates four toothbrushes plus a glass that measures 2⅝ inches at the top and 1¾ inches at the bottom. Before you start making your own holder, select the glass you want to use so you can cut a hole to fit it exactly. Paint the shelf to match the color scheme in your bathroom or cover the surface with three coats of a clear acrylic wood finish, as we did, to show off the grain of the wood. This project utilizes common tools with the exception of the circle cutter, which you will need to make the hole for the cup. Available in most hardware stores for around $12, a circle cutter can cut holes ranging from ⅞ inch to 4 inches in diameter. It is a handy tool to add to your shop.

Clamp the 27⅜-inch-long 1x4 to your workbench and, referring to the Cutting Plan (see Fig. 1), cut the curved shorter pieces first. To lay out the curves, place the point of a compass 1 inch down

MATERIALS LIST

Quantity	Size	Description	Location or Use
1	27⅜ inches	1x4 clear poplar, pine, cedar or cypress	shelf, back & support brackets
1	24 inches	⅝x¾-inch nose & cove molding	trim
1 handful	1¼-inch	galvanized finish nails	
2	2½-inch	#8 brass roundhead screws	back
1 bottle	8 ounces	carpenter's glue	
1 can	10 ounces	water-based wood putty	
1 sheet	60-grit	sandpaper	
1 sheet	120-grit	sandpaper	
1 sheet	220-grit	sandpaper	
1 pint		enamel paint or a clear waterborne acrylic urethane wood finish	

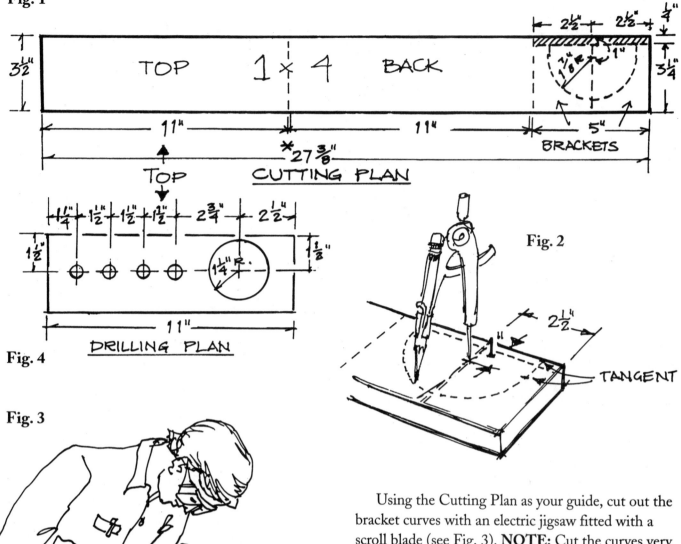

Fig. 1

TOP 1 x 4 BACK

$3\frac{1}{2}$"

$2\frac{1}{2}$" $2\frac{1}{2}$" $\frac{1}{4}$"

$\frac{3}{4}$"

11" 11" 5"

BRACKETS

*$27\frac{3}{8}$"

CUTTING PLAN

Fig. 4

$1\frac{1}{4}$" $1\frac{1}{2}$" $1\frac{1}{2}$" $1\frac{1}{2}$" $2\frac{3}{4}$" $2\frac{1}{2}$"

TOP

$1\frac{1}{2}$"

$1\frac{1}{4}$" R.

$1\frac{1}{2}$"

11"

DRILLING PLAN

Fig. 2

$2\frac{1}{2}$"

1"

TANGENT

Fig. 3

CLAMP

1x4

WORKBENCH

CURVED BRACKET CUT OUT

Using the Cutting Plan as your guide, cut out the bracket curves with an electric jigsaw fitted with a scroll blade (see Fig. 3). **NOTE:** Cut the curves very slowly in order to resist the tendency of the point of the saw blade to wander away from the center of the curve. Also, notice that one leg of each bracket is ¾ inch longer than the other.

Once you have cut out both brackets, sand their curves, using 60-, 120- and 220-grit sandpaper wrapped around a soup can or any similarly shaped object. Cut the remaining length of 1x4 into two 11-inch pieces for the back and the top shelf.

Using the measurements in Fig. 4 as your guide (or making adjustments for your own glass), cut out the toothbrush holes with a ⁹⁄₁₆-inch spade drill and the water glass hole with a hole cutter mounted on a drill press (see Fig. 5). Check to make sure that your glass will fit.

from the side edge of the 1x4 and 2½ inches in from the end (see Fig. 2). Set the compass at a 1⅞-inch radius and draw a 180-degree arc. After scribing this half circle, draw a line, tangent to each end of the arc, continuing ¾ inch toward the side edge of the board (see Figs. 2 & 8).

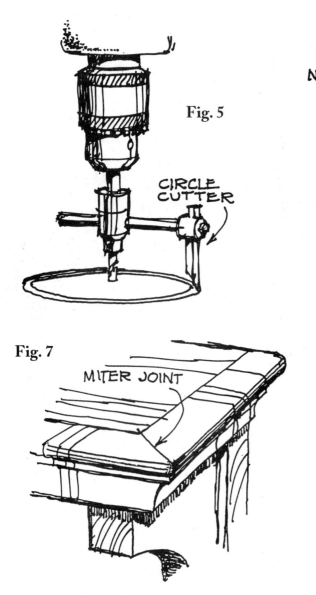

Fig. 5

CIRCLE CUTTER

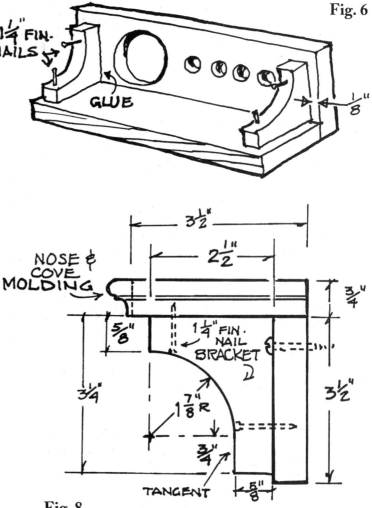

Fig. 6

1¼" FIN. NAILS

GLUE

⅛"

NOSE & COVE MOLDING

3½"

2½"

¾

⅝

1¼" FIN. NAIL BRACKET

3¾

1⅞" R

¾

3½"

⅝"

TANGENT

Fig. 8

Fig. 7

MITER JOINT

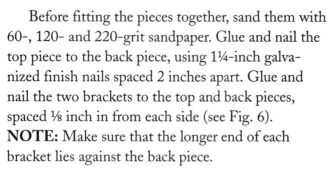

Before fitting the pieces together, sand them with 60-, 120- and 220-grit sandpaper. Glue and nail the top piece to the back piece, using 1¼-inch galvanized finish nails spaced 2 inches apart. Glue and nail the two brackets to the top and back pieces, spaced ⅛ inch in from each side (see Fig. 6). **NOTE:** Make sure that the longer end of each bracket lies against the back piece.

Cut the three ⅝x¾-inch nose-and-cove molding pieces slightly longer than necessary and fine-tune them to fit the shelf perfectly. Hold each molding piece against the shelf edge and make pencil marks for the 45-degree mitered corner cuts, then use a miter box or a table saw to make the cuts. Glue the front molding to the front edge of the top piece. Fit the side moldings to the front molding, and glue them to the sides of the top piece (see Fig. 7). Use clamps or large rubber bands to hold the molding in place while the glue dries.

Countersink all nails, fill the holes with wood putty and give all surfaces a final sanding with 60-, 120- and 220-grit sandpaper. Paint the toothbrush holder with three coats of either an enamel paint or a clear waterborne acrylic urethane wood finish.

Attach the unit to your bathroom wall with two brass screws (see Fig. 8), placed 1 inch down from the top and 1 inch in from the inside of the brackets (see page 16, Attaching to the Wall).

Bread Box

IT'S NO ACCIDENT that this bread box looks like an antique salt box. The salt box was a common kitchen item in the 1800s, mimicking the shape of the Early American "saltbox" house. We like the shape and have taken the liberty of converting it into this bread box, finding it a convenient size for storing pastries and bread and a good way to keep them fresh.

Although any type of plywood can be used, we strongly recommend that you indulge yourself and buy a special veneer plywood, such as birch, bass or even teak (sold in marine supply outlets), to make this project stand out.

The decoration on the top is entirely up to you. Some suggestions are carving a design with a utility knife or dremel tool, hand-painting or stenciling your own design, using press-type or vinyl stick-on letters or burning on a design with an electric wood-burning tool (see Sources).

Begin by cutting out all the pieces of ½-inch plywood, according to the dimensions shown in the Cutting Plan (see Fig. 1). Using a table saw, bevel the top edge of the front piece at a 29-degree angle and the top edge of the back piece at a 42-degree angle (see Fig. 2, Side View). Cut the ⅛-inch plywood into a 9x12-inch rectangle for the bottom

MATERIALS LIST

Quantity	Size	Description	Location or Use
1	13x36 inches	½-inch plywood	front, back, sides, roof
1	9x12 inches	⅛-inch plywood	bottom
1 pair	1x1-inch	solid brass hinges	roof
1 box	1-inch	galvanized wire nails	
1 bottle	8 ounces	carpenter's glue	
1 can	10 ounces	water-based wood putty	
1 sheet	120-grit	sandpaper	
1 sheet	220-grit	sandpaper	
1 pint		clear waterborne acrylic urethane wood finish	

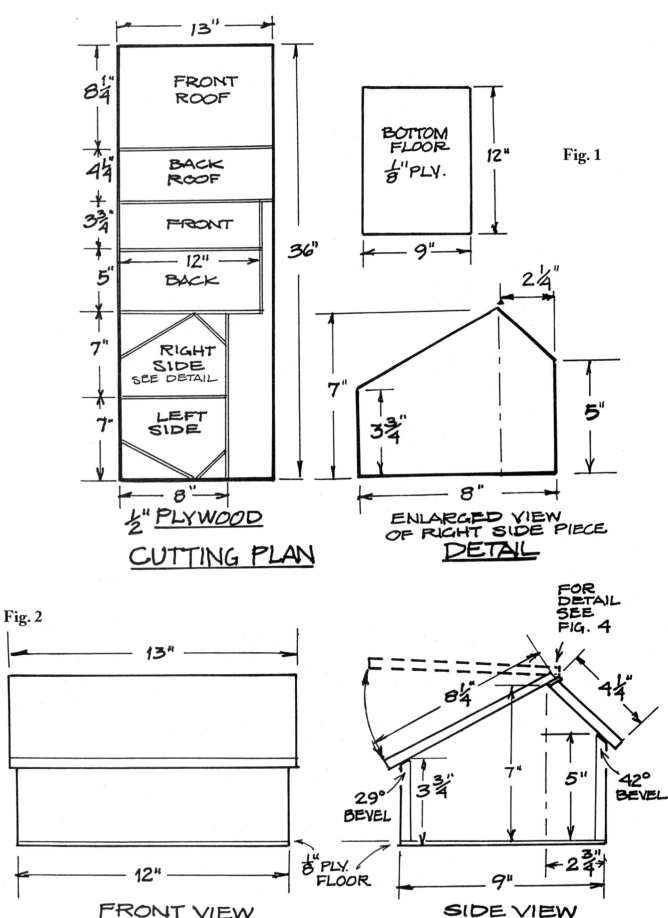

13"

FRONT ROOF

8¼"

BACK ROOF

4¼"

FRONT

3¾"

12"

BACK

5"

RIGHT SIDE
SEE DETAIL

7"

LEFT SIDE

7"

36"

8"

½" PLYWOOD

CUTTING PLAN

BOTTOM FLOOR
⅛" PLY.

12"

9"

Fig. 1

2¼"

7"

3¾"

5"

8"

ENLARGED VIEW
OF RIGHT SIDE PIECE
DETAIL

Fig. 2

13"

12"

FRONT VIEW

FOR DETAIL SEE FIG. 4

8¼"

4¼"

7"

5"

29° BEVEL

3¾"

42° BEVEL

⅛" PLY. FLOOR

9"

2¾"

SIDE VIEW

Fig. 3

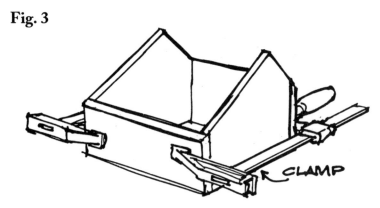

Fig. 4

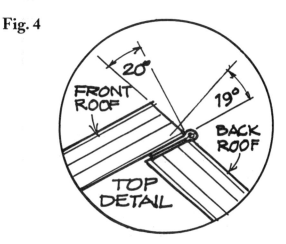

piece. Sand all the inside surfaces, using 120-grit followed by 220-grit sandpaper.

Lay the bottom on your work surface and glue it, the front, the back and the two sides together. Clamp the front and back to the side pieces (see Fig. 3). After the glue has set (20 to 30 minutes), remove the clamps and nail the pieces together, using 1-inch galvanized wire nails, spaced approximately 2 inches apart.

Bevel the top edge of the front roof to a 20-degree angle and the top edge of the back roof to a 19-degree angle (see Fig. 4).

Turn the bread box over on its front face, and glue and nail the back roof on, so that it overlaps the sides by ½ inch.

Position the two hinges 2 inches in from the ends, and score around them with a utility knife. Mortise out where each hinge leaf will go, then

Fig. 5

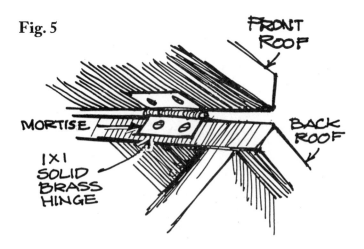

screw the hinges onto the underside of the front roof and to the top edge of the back roof (see Fig. 5).

Sand again, using 220-grit sandpaper, taking special care to smooth the edges and corners.

If you have used a particularly nice type of veneered plywood, we suggest giving the entire bread box a minimum of four coats of a clear waterborne acrylic urethane finish.

Recipe Box

THIS BIRCH RECIPE BOX holds 4x6 index cards and has a slanted front, where you can rest a recipe card and refer to it while you are cooking. The hinged top flips open, making recipes readily accessible, and the box's compact 6x7-inch size does not take up valuable counterspace. If you tend to order in food more than you practice gourmet cooking and don't need a recipe file, use the box instead as a convenient place to store telephone numbers and addresses, computer disks or even photographs. The box is small enough to construct from a leftover piece of plywood, and it is much more appealing than the usual plastic containers available on the market.

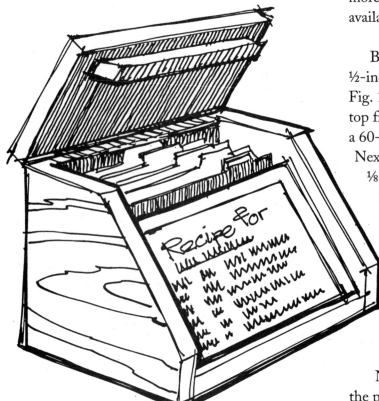

Begin by cutting out all the pieces from the ½-inch plywood, as shown in the Cutting Plan (see Fig. 1). Use a table saw to bevel the top edge of the top front and the bottom edge of the bottom front at a 60-degree angle (see Fig. 2, Section Side View). Next, cut a ⅛-inch-wide and 1/16-inch-deep groove ⅛ inch in from the front edge of the bottom piece to form the slot that will hold the recipe card.

Sand all the surfaces that will face inside the box, using 120- and 220-grit sandpaper. Before gluing the pieces together, temporarily assemble the box, checking to make sure everything fits together snugly (see Fig. 3).

Next, lay the left side face down and mark where the pieces will be glued and joined to it, using a pen-

MATERIALS LIST			
Quantity	**Size**	**Description**	**Location or Use**
1	13¼ x 15⅛ inches	½-inch birch plywood	sides, fronts, back, bottom
1 pair	¾ x 1-inch	solid brass box hinges	top and back
1 bottle	8 ounces	carpenter's glue	
1 sheet	120-grit	sandpaper	
1 sheet	220-grit	sandpaper	
1 pint		clear semigloss waterborne acrylic urethane wood finish	

Fig. 1

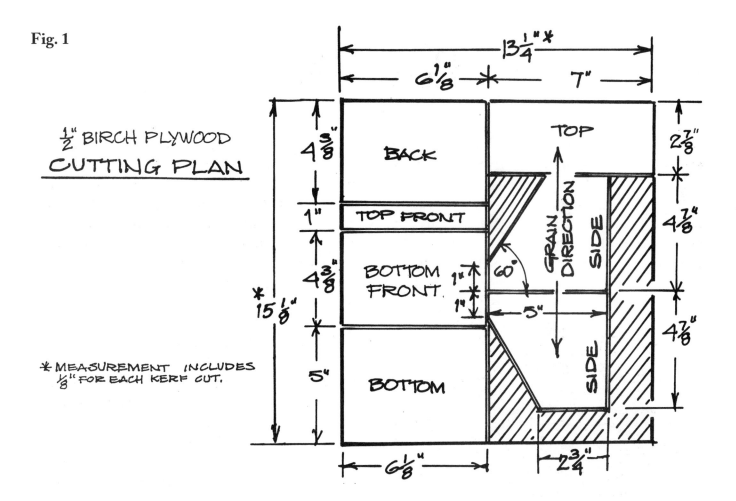

½" BIRCH PLYWOOD
CUTTING PLAN

* MEASUREMENT INCLUDES
⅛" FOR EACH KERF CUT.

cil to draw a light line ½ inch in from the slanted front edge of the side piece (see Fig. 4). Spread a bead of carpenter's glue along this line, along the two inside edges of the side piece and along the bottom edge of the front piece. Carefully position the back, front and bottom pieces together, laying them on top of the glued side piece.

Measure and mark in ⅝ inch from the underneath front edge of the top piece to show where the top front piece will go. Glue the top front to the underneath side of the top piece (see Fig. 5). Before the glue has dried (wait about 10 minutes), put the top in place with the other assembled pieces and check to see that the top front is in line with the bottom front. Place a board or weight on top of these

Fig. 2

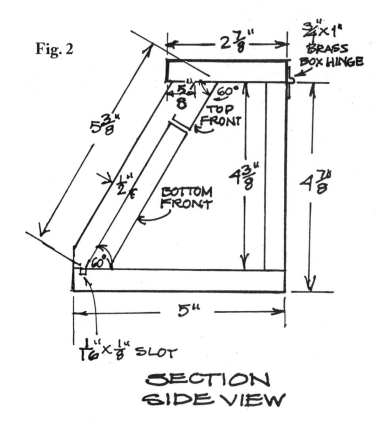

SECTION
SIDE VIEW

Fig. 3

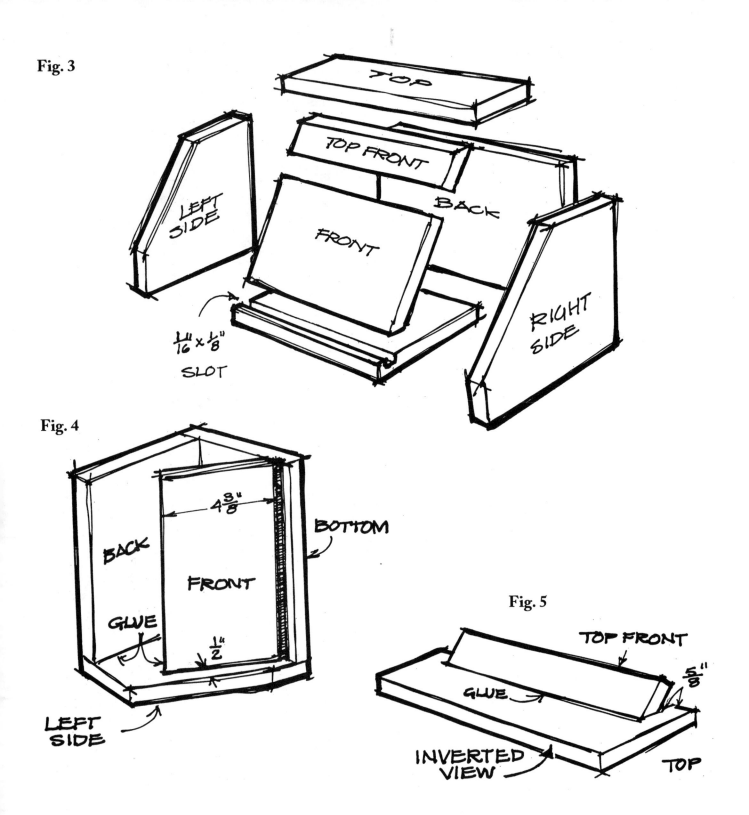

$\frac{1}{16}" \times \frac{1}{8}"$ SLOT

Fig. 4

BACK

$4\frac{3}{8}"$

BOTTOM

FRONT

GLUE

$\frac{1}{2}"$

LEFT SIDE

Fig. 5

TOP FRONT

GLUE

$\frac{5}{8}"$

INVERTED VIEW

TOP

pieces while the glue is drying (about 30 minutes). Turn the assembly over and attach the remaining side piece.

After the glue has dried, screw two ¾x1-inch brass box hinges to the top and back, 1 inch from the outside edges. Sand the exterior surfaces, using 120- and 220-grit sandpaper, and brush on three coats of clear semigloss waterborne acrylic urethane wood finish, sanding after each coat of finish once it's thoroughly dry.

HEIRLOOM CHEST (PAGE 32)

Storage Projects You Can Build

STORAGE STOOL OR OTTOMAN, PORTABLE WRITING DESK,
DESK TRAY, DIVIDED PEN & PENCIL BOX, VCR STORAGE UNIT (PAGES 96, 79, 86, 88 AND 106)

Storage Projects You Can Build

WALL FILE (PAGE 82)

DECK & POOL-CUSHION STORAGE BENCH (PAGE 112)

Storage Projects You Can Build

TENNIS EQUIPMENT STORAGE RACK, COAT, HAT & GLOVE RACK,
TRASH SHED, UNDER-BED STORAGE BOX ON ROLLERS (PAGES 130, 74, 120 AND 28)

WRAPPING & MAILING CENTER, BREAD BOX,
KITCHEN CLEANING CADDY, TOOTHBRUSH & CUP HOLDER (PAGES 91, 43, 66 AND 40)

HOSE HOUSE (PAGES 116)

UNDER-SINK DETERGENT HOLDER, UNDER-SINK TRASH BAG HOLDER,
UNDER-SINK REMOVABLE SHELVES, KITCHEN CLEANING CADDY (PAGES 57, 61, 63 AND 66)

Under-Sink Detergent Holder

SINCE MOST DISHWASHERS are located next to the sink, it makes sense to store dishwasher powder and liquid soap together, within arm's reach. This holder, which screws to the inside of the under-sink cabinet door, provides an easily accessible place for detergents, eliminating the frustration and discomfort of bending over and searching in what is often a damp, dark area underneath the sink. Before you start this project, however, make sure to measure your containers to see if they will fit into the holder described below, designed for a liquid soap bottle that measures 2½x3½x10½ inches and a dishwasher powder box that measures 2x6x9 inches. If not, rework our plans so they fit your needs.

MATERIALS LIST

Quantity	Size	Description	Location or Use
1	13⅝x19⅜ inches	½-inch lauan plywood	sides, front, bottom, back, partition
1 handful	1-inch	wire brads	
4	1-inch	#6 roundhead screws	back
1 bottle	8 ounces	carpenter's glue	
1 sheet	60-grit	sandpaper	
1 sheet	120-grit	sandpaper	
1 sheet	220-grit	sandpaper	
1 can	10 ounces	water-based wood putty	
1 pint		clear waterborne acrylic urethane finish or paint of choice	

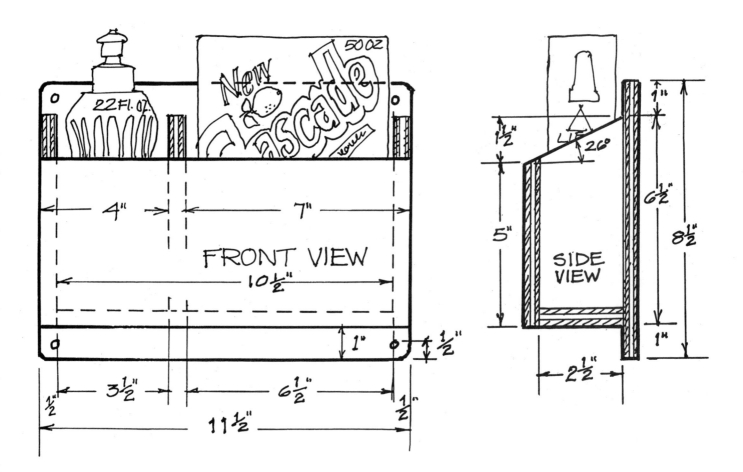

FRONT VIEW

SIDE VIEW

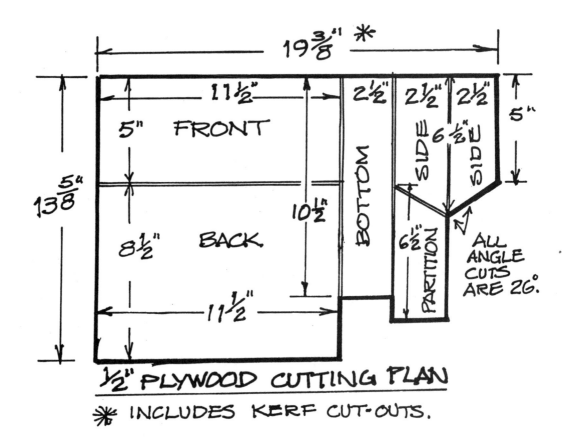

Fig. 1

½" PLYWOOD CUTTING PLAN

✳ INCLUDES KERF CUT-OUTS.

Fig. 2

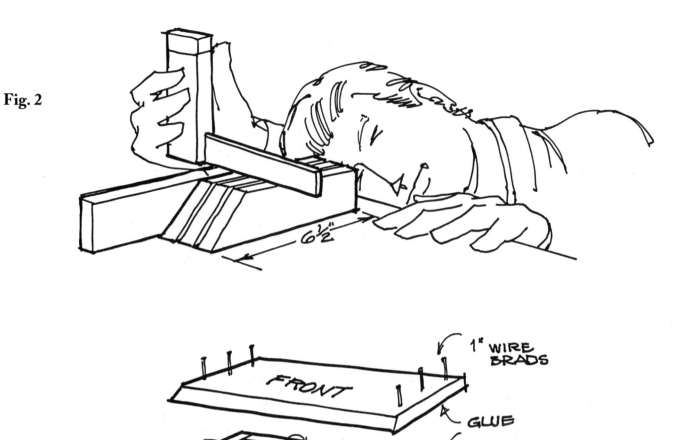

Fig. 3

FRONT

1" WIRE BRADS

GLUE

GLUE

$\frac{1"}{8}$-DIA. MOUNTING HOLE

$6\frac{1}{2}"$

GLUE

$3\frac{1}{2}"$

Cut out all the pieces as shown in the Cutting Plan (see Fig. 1). Place the two sides, the bottom and the partition pieces together to make sure they are exactly the same width (see Fig. 2), and sand down any pieces that do not conform, using 60-grit sandpaper. With a table saw, bevel the top edge of the front piece at a 26-degree angle.

Sand the edges and all surfaces that will face inside the holder until smooth, using 120- and 220-grit sandpaper. To avoid confusion later on, label each piece lightly in pencil on a surface that won't show after the project is assembled.

Drill four ⅛-inch pilot holes, ½ inch in from each edge of the back piece, for the mounting screws (see Fig. 3). Before gluing, temporarily assemble the holder, marking in pencil on the back piece where the sides, partition and bottom pieces will go, and checking for final alignment. The partition piece is 4 inches in from one side and 7 inches in from the other side of the back, and the bottom piece is positioned 1 inch from the bottom edge of the back piece (see Fig. 1, Front View).

When you are sure that all the pieces will fit together perfectly, lay the back piece down and spread a thin layer of glue where you have marked in pencil. Carefully glue the sides, partition and bottom pieces in place. Wait 10 to 15 minutes for the glue to set up, then apply glue to the top edges of the sides, partition and bottom pieces and lay the front piece in place. Apply pressure while the glue is drying by stacking heavy objects (such as paint cans or heavy books) on top of the assembly (see Fig. 4). Once the glue has set up, nail the front to the sides, partition and bottom, using 1-inch wire brads. Then turn the holder over and nail the back to the sides, bottom and partition.

Use a nail set to sink the nail heads below the surface of the wood, and fill the holes with wood putty. Round off all the corners and sand the surfaces smooth, using 60-, 120- and 220-grit sandpaper. Finish with three coats of a clear waterborne acrylic urethane or paint. Screw the under-sink detergent holder to the inside of your kitchen sink cabinet door, using four 1-inch #6 roundhead screws.

Fig. 4

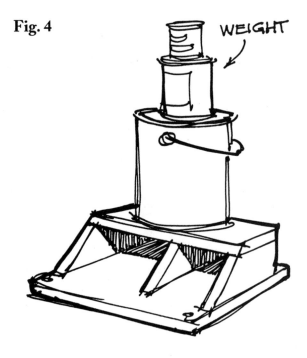

NOTE: If the door is faced with plastic laminate, drill ³⁄₃₂-inch-diameter pilot holes before attaching the screws.

Storage Projects You Can Build

Under-Sink Trash Bag Holder

THIS SIMPLE PROJECT is large enough to hold a 2½x8-inch trash bag box. And, once it's in place, it's high enough that you can easily remove a plastic bag from it without bending over. Measure the size of the cardboard container that your trash bags come in and adjust the measurements given below, if necessary. We attached our unit to the back of the cabinet door below the kitchen sink. Before you actually screw yours into place, be sure to check that its position will allow the door to close.

Cut out all the pieces from the ½-inch plywood, following the dimensions shown on the Cutting Plan (see Fig. 1). Referring to page 59, Fig. 2, check to make sure that the bottom and the two side pieces are exactly the same width (2⅝ inches), and sand down any areas that do not conform, using 60-grit sandpaper. Using a table saw, bevel the top edge of the front piece at a 26-degree angle (see Fig. 2).

Sand the edges and all surfaces that will face inside the holder, using 120- and 220-grit sandpaper.

Drill a ⅛-inch-diameter hole in each corner of the back piece, ¼ inch in from each edge. Place the bottom and two side pieces in position on the back piece and glue them together (see Fig. 2). Wait 10 to 15 minutes, then glue the front piece to the sides and bottom, checking to make sure all parts are aligned correctly.

After the glue has set up, nail the front to the sides and bottom, using 1-inch wire brads (see Fig. 3). Turn the piece over and nail the back to the sides and bottom. Use a nail set to sink the nail heads below the surface of the wood, and fill the holes with wood putty.

MATERIALS LIST

Quantity	Size	Description	Location or Use
1	10x14½ inches	½-inch plywood	back, front, sides, bottom
1 dozen	1-inch	wire brads	
4	1-inch	#6 roundhead screws	back
1 bottle	8 ounces	carpenter's glue	
1 sheet	60-grit	sandpaper	
1 sheet	120-grit	sandpaper	
1 sheet	220-grit	sandpaper	
1 can	10 ounces	water-based wood putty	
1 pint		clear waterborne acrylic urethane finish	

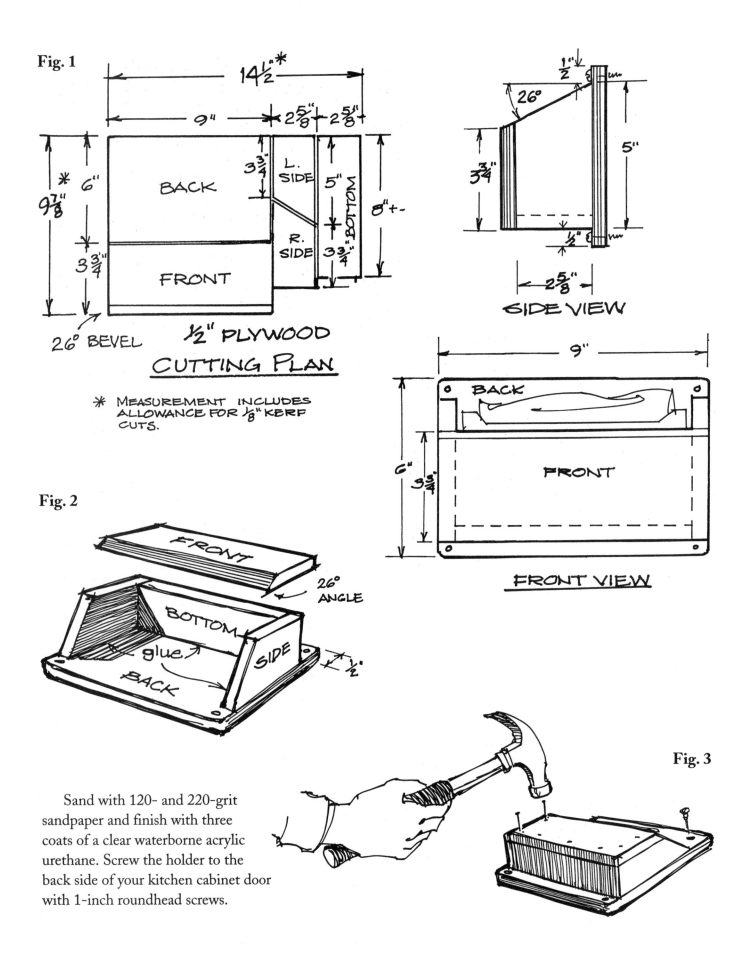

Fig. 1

14½"*

9"

2⅝"   2⅝"

BACK

3¾"

L. SIDE

5" BOTTOM

6"

9⅞"

R. SIDE

3¾"

3¾"

8"+-

FRONT

26° BEVEL

½" PLYWOOD
CUTTING PLAN

* MEASUREMENT INCLUDES
ALLOWANCE FOR ⅛" KERF
CUTS.

SIDE VIEW

½"

26°

3¾"

5"

½"

2⅝"

FRONT VIEW

9"

BACK

6"

9¾"

FRONT

Fig. 2

FRONT

26°
ANGLE

BOTTOM

glue

SIDE

BACK

½"

Fig. 3

Sand with 120- and 220-grit
sandpaper and finish with three
coats of a clear waterborne acrylic
urethane. Screw the holder to the
back side of your kitchen cabinet door
with 1-inch roundhead screws.

Under-Sink Removable Shelves

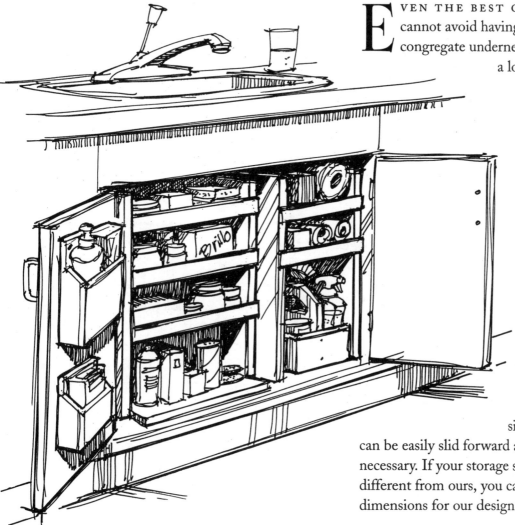

EVEN THE BEST OF KITCHEN DESIGNS cannot avoid having plumbing pipes congregate underneath the sink, resulting in a loss of valuable storage space. The plumber has first priority when it comes to accessibility there. One solution we have found is to build two removable shelving units: One shallow unit sits in front of the pipes and holds cleaning supplies like scouring powder, silver polish and steel wool. A second shelving unit, which is deeper and fits next to the pipes, is designed for paper towels, aluminum foil, wax paper and other similar items. Both units can be easily slid forward and removed if or when necessary. If your storage space and needs are different from ours, you can simply adjust the dimensions for our design to fit your space.

MATERIALS LIST (FOR TWO SHELVING UNITS)

Quantity	Size	Description	Location or Use
1 sheet	4x4 feet	¼-inch A-C plywood	back pieces
1 sheet	4x4 feet	½-inch A-C plywood	sides, shelves & bottom foot plate
1	6 feet	¼x1½-inch lattice	shelf fronts
1 box	1⅛-inch	galvanized wire nails	
1 bottle	8 ounces	carpenter's glue	
1 pint		clear waterborne acrylic urethane wood finish or paint of choice	

Fig. 1

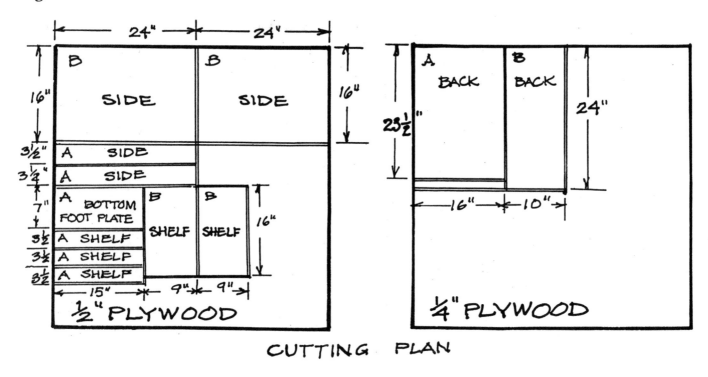

CUTTING PLAN

Measure the space underneath your sink and figure out what the dimensions should be for both units. **NOTE:** When taking measurements, remember to account for the width of the cabinet doors underneath your sink, since the units need to be able to clear them when they are removed.

Referring to the Cutting Plan (see Fig. 1) and making any adjustments, if necessary, cut out the 10x24-inch and 16x23½-inch back pieces from the ¼-inch plywood and the four sides, five shelves and bottom foot plate from the ½-inch plywood.

To make the shallow unit (A), which will stand in front of the exposed pipes, glue and nail, using 1⅛-inch galvanized wire nails, the back piece to the two side pieces, leaving a ½-inch space at the base to fit the bottom foot plate. After the glue has dried, measure and mark where the three plywood shelves should be positioned to hold your supplies, and glue and nail them in place between the two sides. To prevent supplies from toppling forward off the shelves, cover the front edges with ¼x1½-inch lattice pieces, glued and nailed to the shelf edges and the front edge of the sides (see Fig. 2).

Because the unit can become top-heavy after it is filled with supplies, we cut a foot plate out of ½-inch plywood to extend out approximately 1¼ inches beyond the front and 2 inches beyond the back of the sides of the unit (see Fig. 2). Insert the foot plate between the two sides of the unit and glue and nail the sides to the foot plate.

Before you start building the second unit, put the first unit in place and check the measurements of the remaining available space.

To make the deep shelving unit (B), which fits under the sink and next to the plumbing pipes, glue and nail the back piece to the two side pieces, again using 1⅛-inch galvanized wire nails. After the glue has dried, measure and mark where the two shelves will be positioned. Lay the unit on one side, place a bead of glue on the side and back edges of the shelves and carefully slide the two shelves in place. After that glue has partially dried, hammer 1⅛-inch wire nails, spaced every 3 inches, through the sides and into the edges of the shelves. Cover the front edges of the shelves with strips of lattice to keep supplies from falling out. Glue and nail the strips, using

Fig. 2

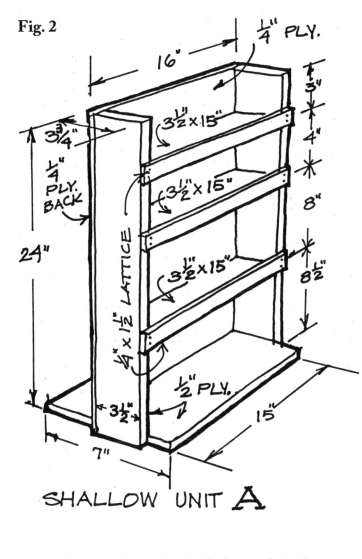

1/4" PLY.

16"

3 3/4"

1/4" PLY. BACK

24"

3 1/2" x 15"

3"

4"

8"

8 1/2"

3 1/2" x 15"

3 1/2" x 15"

1/4" x 1 1/2" LATTICE

1/2" PLY.

3 1/2"

7"

15"

SHALLOW UNIT A

Fig. 3

1/4" PLY.

10"

9"x16" SHELF

SIDE

24"

1/2" PLY.

1/4"x1 1/2" LATTICE

4"

5"

15"

9"

16"

DEEP UNIT B

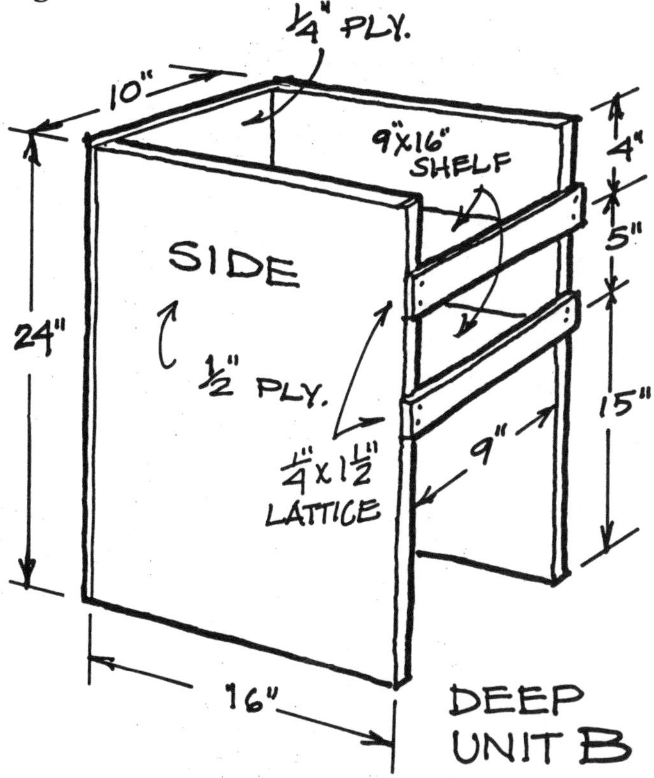

NOTE:

DIMENSIONS SHOWN HERE MAY NOT FIT YOUR SITUATION. CHECK BEFORE CUTTING YOUR PLYWOOD.

1⅛-inch wire nails, to the shelf edges and the front edge of the sides. The bottom of the unit is left open to allow the Kitchen Cleaning Caddy (see page 66) to slide in and out.

We finished both units with three coats of a clear waterborne acrylic urethane to facilitate cleaning off finger marks and dirt. However, you may want to paint yours to match the color of your kitchen cabinets.

Under-Sink Removable Shelves

Kitchen Cleaning Caddy

WHETHER YOU ARE waxing the car or washing windows, this portable cleaning caddy can eliminate many steps back and forth from the house to your work site. It's big enough to store a wide variety of cleaning supplies, yet small enough to fit in a broom closet or neatly under the sink. In fact, we included a space for it in one of the earlier projects (see page 63, Under-Sink Removable Shelves).

Referring to the Cutting Plan (see Fig. 1), mark and cut out the pieces from the ½-inch plywood.

To make the hole for the handle in the center divider, you'll need a ½-inch-diameter spade drill bit, an electric drill and an electric jigsaw fitted with a scroll saw blade. First, mark the shape and size of the handle on the center divider according to the dimensions shown in Fig. 1, Side View. Then drill two ½-inch-diameter holes at both of the lower corners of the handle. Place the blade of your jigsaw in one of the holes and cut out the handle hole (see Fig. 2). Sand all the inside surfaces with 60-, 120- and 220-grit sandpaper.

To assemble the side and end pieces, glue and nail the sides to the ends, using 1⅛-inch galvanized wire nails spaced 2 inches apart. Check to make sure that the box is perfectly square, then trace the outside edge of the box bottom onto the ⅛-inch plywood (see Fig. 3) and cut out this piece. Glue and nail the bottom to the side and end pieces, using 1⅛-inch galvanized wire nails.

To attach the center divider/handle, draw two parallel lines, ½ inch apart, on the inside center of the bottom and end pieces. Spread a thin bead of

MATERIALS LIST			
Quantity	**Size**	**Description**	**Location or Use**
1	17⅛x31¼ inches	½-inch plywood	sides, ends & divider/handle
1	8½x16 inches	⅛-inch plywood	bottom
1 box	1⅛-inch	galvanized wire nails	
1 bottle	8 ounces	carpenter's glue	
1 can	10 ounces	water-based wood putty	
1 sheet	60-grit	sandpaper	
1 sheet	120-grit	sandpaper	
1 sheet	220-grit	sandpaper	
1 pint		clear waterborne acrylic urethane wood finish	

glue between the lines and stand the box on end. To avoid smearing the glue, hold the handle at an angle as you insert it in the box, carefully twist it into a vertical position, then press it into the bead of glue, checking to make sure it is placed correctly (see Fig. 4). Nail it through the two ends and the bottom to hold it in place, using 1⅛-inch nails. Use a nail set to sink all the nails below the wood's surface, and fill the holes with wood putty.

Sand all the outside edges and surfaces with 60-, 120- and 220-grit sandpaper and brush on three coats of a finish of your choice.

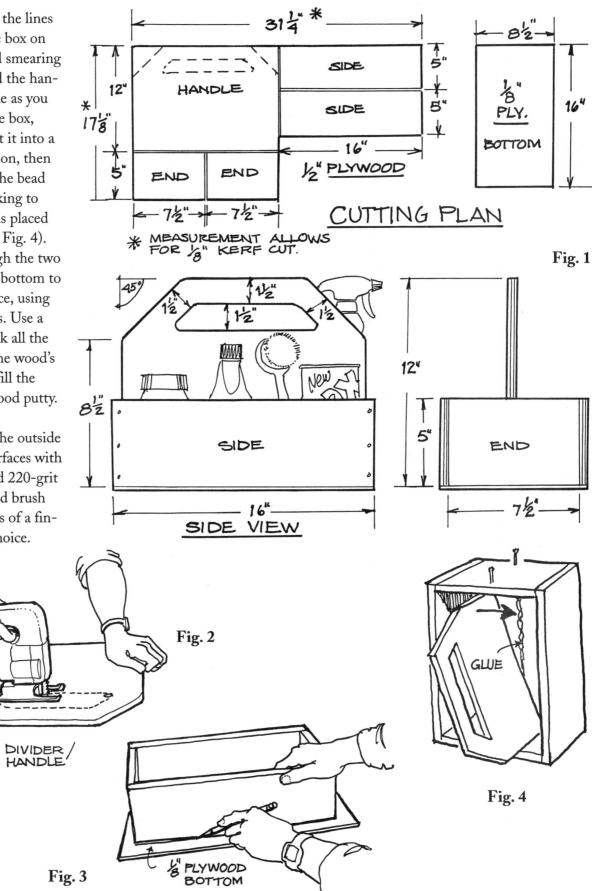

CUTTING PLAN

* MEASUREMENT ALLOWS FOR ⅛" KERF CUT.

Fig. 1

SIDE VIEW

Fig. 2

Fig. 3

Fig. 4

Kitchen Island

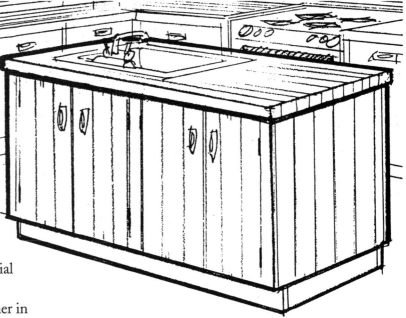

OUR KITCHEN island, pictured on the cover of this book, is easier to build than you might think. If you choose Corian for the top surface, as shown in the photograph, the most difficult part is cutting the hole for the sink. We recommend that you hire a professional to handle this part and install the top later yourself. To avoid this problem altogether, choose another surface material, such as butcher block (which we've used in the project below), plastic laminate or copper sheeting. Use your existing kitchen decor and budget to help you determine what material will serve you best. If you are considering the possibility of installing a sink and/or dishwasher in

Fig. 1

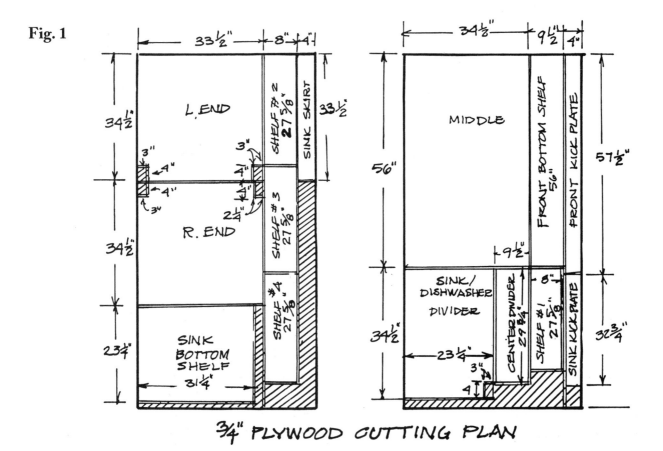

3/4" PLYWOOD CUTTING PLAN

MATERIALS LIST

Quantity	Size	Description	Location or Use
2 sheets	4x8 feet	¾-inch plywood	frame
1	1½x36x60 inches	butcher block	top surface
8	8 feet	1x6 clear T&G cedar	sides, front doors
6	26½ inches	1x8 clear T&G cedar	rear doors
4	27⅝ inches	1x2 cedar	shelf edging (optional)
2	30½ inches	1x2 cedar	side front uprights
1	¾x2x30½ inches	1x3 cedar	center front upright
2	26½ inches	1x2 cedar	rear door uprights
2	8 feet	5⁄4x6 #2 pine	battens
6 pairs	2x2-inch	butt hinges	doors
6	1½x1½-inch	angle brackets	counter support
6		nylon roller friction catches	doors
6	3- to 4-inch	handles with screws	doors
1 box	1-inch	#10 screws	battens
1 box	¾-inch	#8 screws	angle brackets
1 box	1½-inch	#6 galvanized deck screws	shelves & frame
1 box	1½-inch	galvanized finish nails	
1 bottle	8 ounces	waterproof glue	
1 can	10 ounces	water-based wood putty	
1 sheet	60-grit	sandpaper	
1 sheet	120-grit	sandpaper	
1 sheet	220-grit	sandpaper	
1 quart		clear waterborne acrylic urethane finish or a stain of your choice	

your island, be sure to consult your plumber first about running pipes through the floor underneath.

The kitchen island provides an ideal work surface as well as a convenient spot to rest the grocery bags while you unload them. The cabinets hold kitchen staples and glassware.

Begin by building the plywood frame. Cut out all the plywood pieces, as shown in the Cutting Plan (see Fig. 1). With the help of an assistant, stand up the middle piece between the two end pieces, positioning it 23¼ inches in from the rear (see Fig. 2). Check with a carpenter's square to make sure the middle piece is at right angles to the ends. Screw the end pieces to the middle piece, using 1½-inch galvanized deck screws.

Nail the front kick plate to the bottom notches of the end pieces, using 1½-inch galvanized finish nails (see Fig. 3). Next, nail the front bottom shelf to the kick plate and to the end pieces. Position the center divider so it is equidistant from both end pieces on the front side, then glue it to the bottom shelf and middle piece. Secure it by nailing through the back of the middle piece into the center divider, using 1½-inch galvanized finish nails.

Position the sink/dishwasher divider 24 inches over from the left rear end piece (see Fig. 4) and nail

Fig. 2

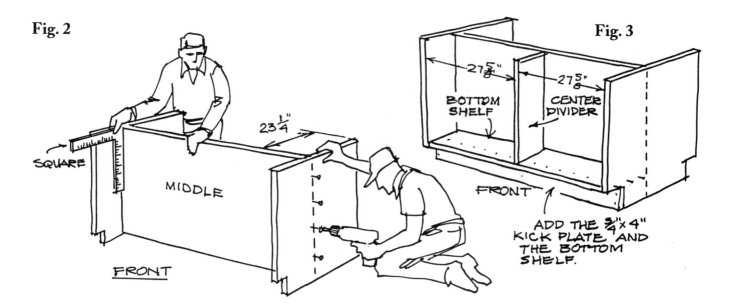

Fig. 3

SQUARE

MIDDLE

$23\frac{1}{4}$"

FRONT

$27\frac{5}{8}$" $27\frac{5}{8}$"

BOTTOM SHELF   CENTER DIVIDER

FRONT

ADD THE $\frac{3}{4}$"x 4" KICK PLATE AND THE BOTTOM SHELF.

it in place, using 1½-inch galvanized finish nails. Nail the sink kick plate to the bottom notches of the wall divider and the right rear end piece. Note that there is no kick plate where the dishwasher will go. Nail the sink bottom shelf to the kick plate, the end piece and the divider.

To hold the butcher block counter in place, screw six 1½x1½-inch metal angle brackets to the inside corners of the frame, using ¾-inch #8 screws (see Fig. 4). Position the butcher block on top of the unit and screw the brackets to the underneath side of the countertop.

Fig. 4

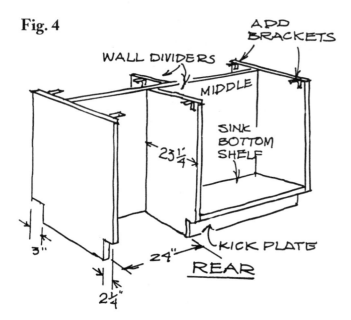

ADD BRACKETS

WALL DIVIDERS

MIDDLE

SINK BOTTOM SHELF

$23\frac{1}{4}$"

3"

24"

$2\frac{1}{4}$"

KICK PLATE

REAR

Space the four 8-inch-wide shelves for the front side according to your own particular needs and nail them through the end pieces and the center divider (see Fig. 5). **NOTE:** It will be necessary to "toe-nail" two of the shelves through the center divider (see Fig. 6). If desired, glue 1x2 cedar trim to the front edges of the shelves to hide the plywood edges.

Cut four of the 8-foot clear T&G cedar 1x6s into 12 boards, each 30½ inches long. Cut the "tongue" off one of the 1x6s and glue and nail this board to the right end of the island, making it flush with the front edge (see Fig. 5). Continue adding pieces of T&G cedar, lightly tapping the tongue of each piece into the groove of the previous one, using a scrap block of wood, until you reach the other side of the unit. Scribe where the last piece of 1x6 overlaps the end of the island, cut off the overlapping piece and glue and nail the boards in place, using 1½-inch finish nails spaced 2 inches apart. Follow the same procedure for the opposite end of the island.

Cut the four remaining 1x6 T&G cedar boards into 12 more 30½-inch lengths to build four doors for the front of the island. Each door is 30½ inches high and 13½ inches wide (see Fig. 7, Front View). Use wider, 1x8 T&G cedar to build the two rear doors, each 26½ inches high and 15¼ inches wide (see Fig. 7, Rear View). Use the ⁵⁄₄x6 #2 pine to make 14½-inch-long battens for the backs of the

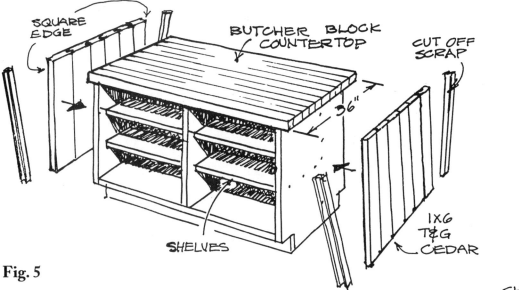

SQUARE EDGE

BUTCHER BLOCK COUNTERTOP

CUT OFF SCRAP

36"

SHELVES

1X6 T&G CEDAR

Fig. 5

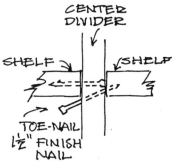

CENTER DIVIDER

SHELF

SHELF

TOE-NAIL 1½" FINISH NAIL

Fig. 6

Fig. 7

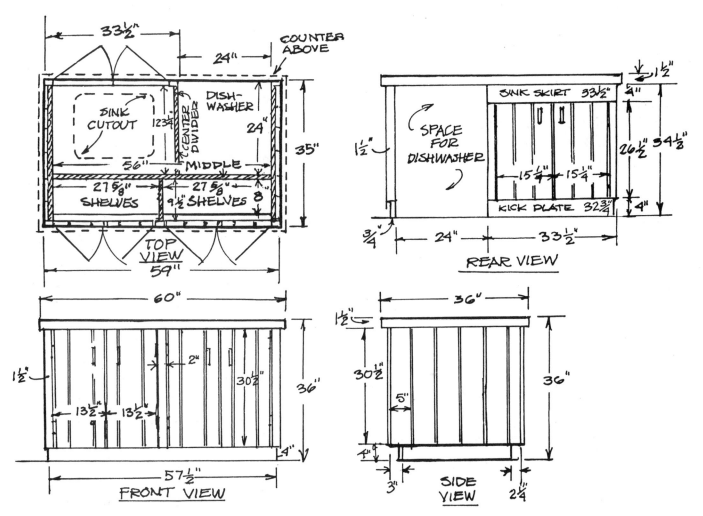

33½"

24"

COUNTER ABOVE

SINK CUTOUT

12¾"

DISH-WASHER 24"

CENTER DIVIDER

MIDDLE

35"

56"

27⅝" SHELVES

27⅝" SHELVES

9½"

8

TOP VIEW 59"

60"

1½"

2"

30½"

36"

13½"

13½"

4"

57½"

FRONT VIEW

1½"

1½"

¾"

SINK SKIRT 33½"

SPACE FOR DISHWASHER

15¼"

15¼"

26½" 34⅛"

KICK PLATE 32¾"

4"

¾"

24"

33½"

REAR VIEW

36"

1½"

30½"

36"

5"

4"

3"

SIDE VIEW

2¼"

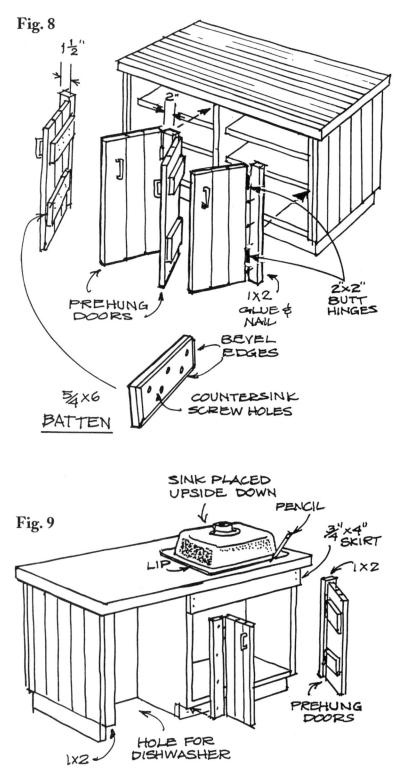

Fig. 8

1½"

2"

PREHUNG
DOORS

1X2
GLUE &
NAIL

2"x2"
BUTT
HINGES

BEVEL
EDGES

⁵⁄₄x6
BATTEN

COUNTERSINK
SCREW HOLES

Fig. 9

SINK PLACED
UPSIDE DOWN

PENCIL

LIP

¾"x4"
SKIRT

1X2

PREHUNG
DOORS

HOLE FOR
DISHWASHER

1X2

sional look, countersink the screws and fill the holes with wood putty.

To hide the bottom of the sink once it is installed, a sink skirt is attached to the rear of the island, spanning the top of the under-sink cabinet. Glue and nail this 4x33½-inch plywood piece so it is flush with the top of the frame (see Fig. 9).

Attach each of the front end doors to the 1x2 cedar front uprights, using 2x2-inch butt hinges, and then glue and nail the door assembly to the island frame, using 1½-inch galvanized finish nails, spaced 3 inches apart (see Fig. 8). The center front doors are attached in the same manner to a 30½-inch 1x3, cut to a width of 2 inches. Follow the same procedure for the rear doors, using two 26½-inch 1x2 cedar uprights. Attaching the doors to the uprights first, rather than attaching the uprights to the unit and then attaching the hinges and the doors to the uprights, saves a great deal of time and allows you to easily align the doors while you are installing them. Attach a nylon roller friction catch inside each of the doors and screw a handle to the front of each as well.

To cut the hole for the sink, lay the sink upside-down and trace around its perimeter (see Fig. 9). Measure the width of the sink's lip, subtract this measurement from the traced perimeter and mark the cutting line. Drill a ⅜-inch starting hole anywhere within the perimeter and cut out the sink hole, using an electric jigsaw.

Fill any exposed nail holes with wood putty, and sand the kitchen island, using 60-, 120- and 220-grit sandpaper. Seal the cedar with a clear waterborne acrylic urethane or a stain of your choice.

Call the plumber to install the sink, faucet and dishwasher.

doors to stiffen them and keep them from warping. Slightly bevel the edges of the battens at a 45-degree angle. Glue and screw them horizontally across the backs of the doors, using 1-inch #10 screws (see Fig. 8). **NOTE:** Space the battens so they will not touch the shelves when the doors are closed. For a profes-

Office &
Entertainment
Storage

Coat, Hat & Glove Rack

HERE'S A PROJECT you can "hang your hat on" . . . and your coat and your gloves, and anything else you can store in a 5x30-inch compartment. This practical solution for extra storage space can be painted or given three coats of a clear acrylic finish. Made from a single 14-foot-long piece of 1x6 pine, with some attractive brass hardware and classical trim, it looks terrific in a front hallway, foyer, mudroom or even a guest room.

From the 14-foot pine 1x6, mark and cut two 30-inch-long pieces for the back and bottom shelf,

MATERIALS LIST

Quantity	Size	Description	Location or Use
2	30 inches	1x6 #2 pine	back & bottom shelf
1	29⅞ inches	1x6 #2 pine	front
1	31½ inches	1x6 #2 pine	top
1	27 inches	1x6 #2 pine	end pieces
1	30 inches	1x2 #2 pine	top shelf support
1 pair	1⅜x2-inch	solid brass hinges	front & bottom shelf
1	48-inch strip	⅝-inch cove bead molding	
1	1½-inch-diameter	wood pull	front
4	3½-inch	Shaker pegs	
1		nylon roller spring catch	
1 box	1½-inch	finish nails	
1 bottle	8 ounces	carpenter's glue	
2	2½-inch	#8 drywall screws	mounting screws
4	1½-inch	#6 drywall screws	mounting screws
1 sheet	60-grit	sandpaper	
1 sheet	120-grit	sandpaper	
1 sheet	220-grit	sandpaper	
1 can	10 ounces	water-based wood putty	
1 pint		semigloss paint or clear waterborne acrylic urethane wood finish	

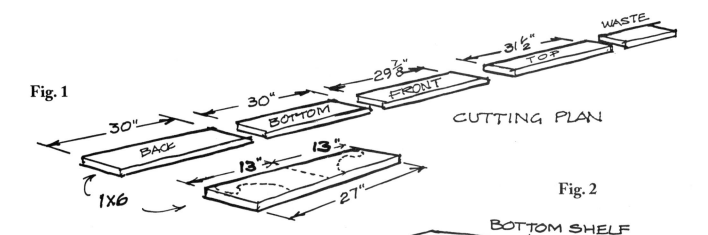

Fig. 1

30" BACK

1X6

30" BOTTOM

29⅞" FRONT

31½" TOP

WASTE

CUTTING PLAN

13" 13"

27"

Fig. 2

BOTTOM SHELF

2"x 1⅜" hinge

4½"

1/16"

FRONT PIECE

Fig. 3

1/16"

1/16"

FRONT

END

BACK

GLUE & NAIL

Fig. 4

TOP

COVE BEAD MOLDING

45° MITER

one 29⅞-inch-long piece for the front, one 31½-inch-long piece for the top shelf and two 13-inch-long pieces for the ends (see Fig. 1). **NOTE:** Make sure the back and bottom shelf are *exactly* the same length.

Referring to Fig. 6 (Side View Section), make a 4⅝-inch arc 1¾ inches up from the bottom of one of the 13-inch end pieces. At the bottom opposite corner of the board, scribe a ⅞-inch-radius circle. Trace the curved pattern onto the other end piece and cut out the shapes, using an electric jigsaw fitted with a scroll saw blade. Sand the curves with 60-, 120- and 220-grit sandpaper.

Screw one leaf of each of the brass hinges onto the bottom shelf, positioning it 4½ inches in from each end (see Fig. 2). Attach the other leaf of each hinge to the front piece, making sure the ends of the bottom shelf extend 1/16 inch beyond the ends of the front piece. **NOTE:** The hinges are attached at this point because it would be difficult to screw them on once the unit is assembled.

Position the hinged front and bottom shelf and the two end pieces and back piece in place. For clearance, the front piece must be 1/16 inch below the top edge of the end pieces (see Fig. 3). Shave or sand the front piece down until there's a 1/16-inch gap. Glue the hinged front and bottom shelf and the two end pieces to the back piece, and hold the pieces together with bar clamps and 1½-inch finish nails. Glue, clamp and nail the top piece to the top of the two end pieces.

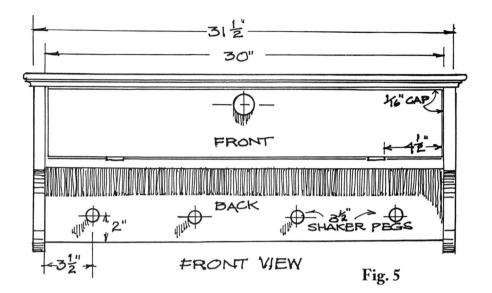

FRONT VIEW

Fig. 5

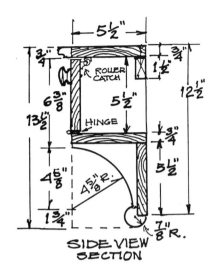

SIDE VIEW
SECTION

Fig. 6

NYLON ROLLER
SPRING CATCH

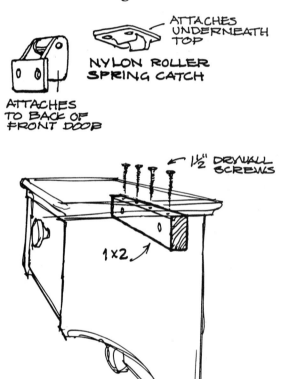

Fig. 7

Measure and cut two pieces of ⅝-inch cove molding for the ends of the top, making 45-degree miter cuts at the corners. Glue the end molding in place. When the glue has dried sufficiently (approximately 20 minutes), measure and cut the front piece of cove molding for the front edge of the top, again making 45-degree miter cuts at the corners (see Fig. 4). Glue it in place.

Locate the center of the front piece and drill a ³⁄₁₆-inch-diameter hole 1½ inches down from the top. Screw in a 1½-inch wood pull (see Fig. 5).

To mark where the Shaker pegs should be positioned, measure 3½ inches in from each side and 2 inches up from the bottom edge of the back piece. Divide the distance between these two points into thirds, so you have four peg locations, equally spaced apart (see Fig. 5). Drill a ½-inch-diameter hole at each location and glue a Shaker peg into each hole.

To keep the front hinged door closed, install a nylon roller spring catch in the top/center of the back side of the door and the underneath center of the top piece of the unit (see Fig. 6).

Fill any nail holes with wood putty, and sand the storage unit using 60-, 120- and 220-grit sandpaper. The coat, hat & glove rack can either be painted with three coats of a semigloss paint or covered with three coats of a urethane finish.

To hang the rack, cut a 30-inch-long piece of 1x2 and screw it to your wall, using two 2½-inch #8 drywall screws drilled into the wall studs (see page 16, Attaching to the Wall). Place the rack on top of this 1x2 ledge (see Fig. 7), screwing it down from the top with four 1½-inch #6 drywall screws.

Eyeglass Holder

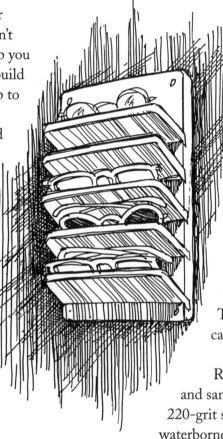

How can you find your misplaced glasses if you don't have your glasses on to help you look for them? One solution is to build this simple rack, which can hold up to five pairs of glasses. Since you may be keeping this in a visible spot and using it often, select plywood with a nice veneer, such as birch, bass, mahogany or teak. To protect the lenses of your eyeglasses, line the inside face of each ledge with velvet, felt or a self-adhesive flocking paper.

Begin by cutting the 6½x12-inch back piece out of the ½-inch plywood. Then cut the five 6½x 2½-inch ledge pieces out of the ¼-inch plywood (see Fig. 1, Cutting Plan).

To make the notches in the back piece where the ¼-inch ledges are inserted, set your table saw at a 40-degree angle. Measure and make a mark 1 inch up from the bottom of the back piece, then make four more marks, each 2 inches apart. Practice with a scrap piece of ½-inch plywood to get the height of the saw blade set so it cuts only halfway through the wood, at a 40-degree angle. Then take the back piece and hold it against the miter gauge of the table saw, making several 40-degree cuts at each mark, until each cut is ¼ inch wide and ¼ inch deep (see Fig. 2). The ledges should fit snugly, so take care not to cut the notches too wide.

Round off all the corners and edges and sand the wooden surfaces, using 120- and 220-grit sandpaper. Apply three coats of a clear waterborne acrylic urethane wood finish to all parts of the project. Before attaching the five ledge

MATERIALS LIST

Quantity	Size	Description	Location or Use
1	6½x12 inches	½-inch veneer plywood	back
1	6½x13 inches	¼-inch veneer plywood	ledges
1	6½x12 inches	velvet, felt or self-adhesive flocking paper	ledges
4	1½-inch	#6 drywall screws & plastic wall anchors	mounting screws
1 bottle	8 ounces	carpenter's glue	ledges
1 sheet	120-grit	sandpaper	
1 sheet	220- grit	sandpaper	
1 pint		clear waterborne acrylic urethane wood finish	

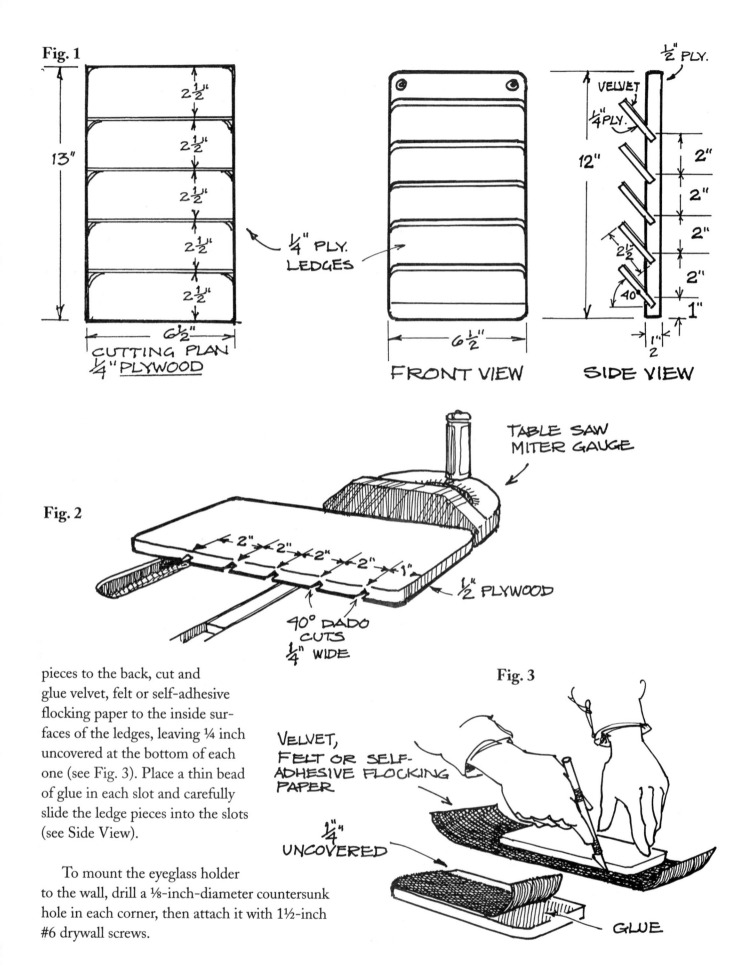

Fig. 1

2½"
2½"
2½"
2½"
2½"

13"

6½"

CUTTING PLAN
¼" PLYWOOD

¼" PLY.
LEDGES

FRONT VIEW

6½"

½" PLY.

VELVET

¼" PLY.

12"

2"
2"
2"
2"
1"

2½"

40°

½"

SIDE VIEW

Fig. 2

TABLE SAW
MITER GAUGE

2" 2" 2" 2" 1"

½" PLYWOOD

40° DADO
CUTS
¼" WIDE

pieces to the back, cut and glue velvet, felt or self-adhesive flocking paper to the inside surfaces of the ledges, leaving ¼ inch uncovered at the bottom of each one (see Fig. 3). Place a thin bead of glue in each slot and carefully slide the ledge pieces into the slots (see Side View).

To mount the eyeglass holder to the wall, drill a ⅛-inch-diameter countersunk hole in each corner, then attach it with 1½-inch #6 drywall screws.

Fig. 3

VELVET,
FELT OR SELF-
ADHESIVE FLOCKING
PAPER

¼"
UNCOVERED

GLUE

Portable Writing Desk

T HIS PORTABLE WRITING desk is lightweight and comfortable to work at. It contains a hinged compartment for stationery and envelopes, plus two open sections at the top, one for letters, bills and stamps, and another with holes for pens and pencils. Sleek and simple in design, it is just the right size to put on your lap if you feel like working from a lawn chair in your backyard. This project can be completed in just a few hours.

Begin by cutting out the pieces from the ½-inch plywood, using the dimensions shown on the Cutting Plan (see Fig. 1). Label the exterior sides of the pieces and sand the interior surfaces, using 60-, 120- and 220-grit sandpaper.

Cut out the 15x16-inch bottom piece from the ⅛-inch plywood and glue the ½x14-inch front piece onto the top front edge of the bottom, leaving a

½-inch space at each end. Do the same with the back piece, gluing it to the top back edge of the bottom. Next, glue the sides to the front and back pieces (see Fig. 2). Make sure all four pieces are perfectly aligned, clamp them together and allow the glue to set for 20 minutes.

While the glue is drying, bevel the inside of the top edge of the 4x14-inch rear divider to a 17-degree angle, using a rasp or block plane and 60-grit sandpaper on a block (see Fig. 3). This is where the

MATERIALS LIST

Quantity	Size	Description	Location or Use
1	23¼ x 24½ inches	½-inch bass plywood	top, sides, front, back, dividers, support blocks, pen & pencil holder
1	15x16 inches	⅛-inch birch plywood or hardboard	bottom piece
1	14-inch strip	½-inch half-round molding	lip/opener
1 pair	1x2-inch	brass butt hinges	
1 bottle	8 ounces	carpenter's glue	
1 sheet	60-grit	sandpaper	
1 sheet	120-grit	sandpaper	
1 sheet	220-grit	sandpaper	
1 pint		clear waterborne acrylic urethane wood finish	

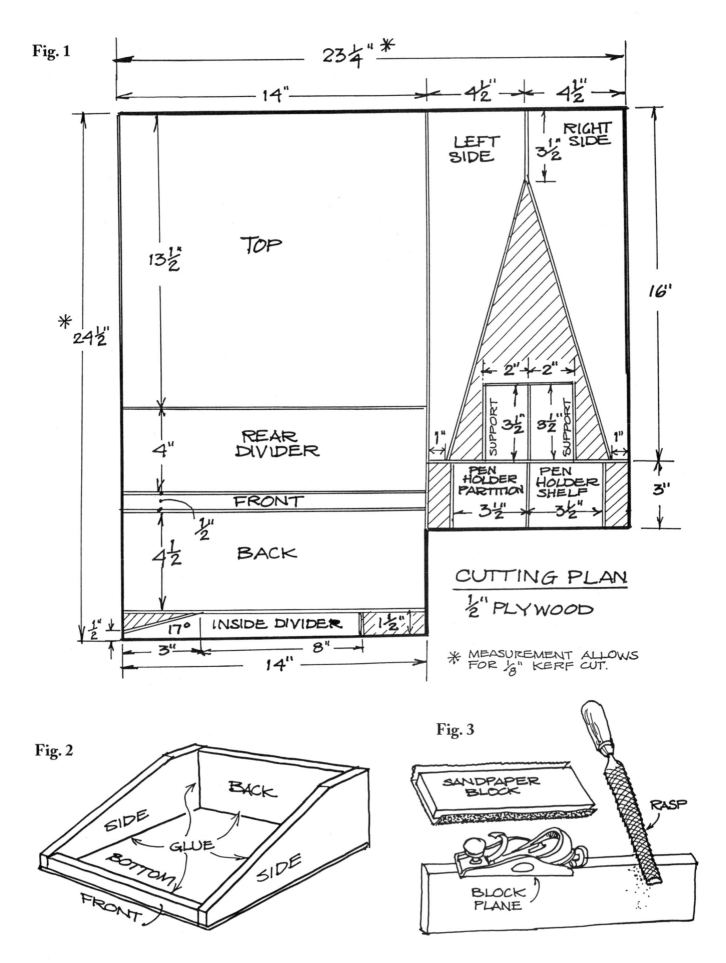

Fig. 1

23¼" *

14"   4½"   4½"

LEFT SIDE   RIGHT SIDE

3½"

TOP

13½"

16"

24½" *

REAR DIVIDER

4"

2"   2"

SUPPORT   SUPPORT

3½"   3½"

1"   1"

FRONT

½"

BACK

4½"

PEN HOLDER PARTITION

PEN HOLDER SHELF

3½"   3½"

3"

½"

17°   INSIDE DIVIDER   1½"

3"   8"

14"

CUTTING PLAN
½" PLYWOOD

* MEASUREMENT ALLOWS FOR ⅛" KERF CUT.

Fig. 2

BACK

SIDE

GLUE

BOTTOM

SIDE

FRONT

Fig. 3

SANDPAPER BLOCK

RASP

BLOCK PLANE

Fig. 4   **Fig. 5**

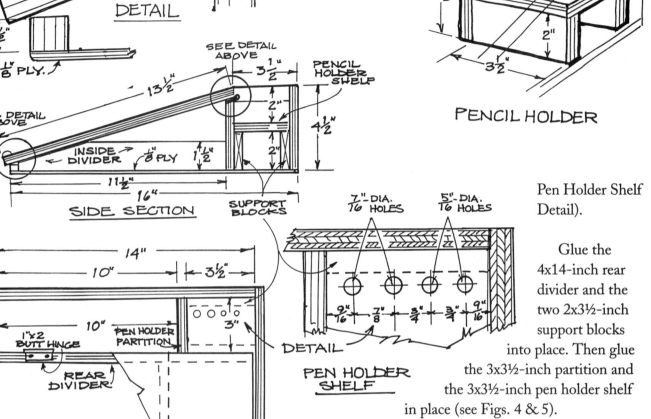

DETAIL

SIDE SECTION

PENCIL HOLDER

TOP VIEW

PEN HOLDER SHELF

Pen Holder Shelf Detail).

Glue the 4x14-inch rear divider and the two 2x3½-inch support blocks into place. Then glue the 3x3½-inch partition and the 3x3½-inch pen holder shelf in place (see Figs. 4 & 5).

Sand and glue the 1½x11-inch inside divider to the bottom, the front and the rear divider, 9 inches in from the left side (see Fig. 4, Top View). Be sure the slanted edge is facing forward.

Test-fit the top piece and sand it off if necessary, so that it just clears the sides when it is opened and closed. Glue and clamp the ½x14-inch half-round molding to the top front (see opening illustration).

Screw the pair of 1x2-inch hinges to the bottom of the top and to the top edge of the rear divider. Sand the outside with 60-, 120- and 220-grit sandpaper and brush on a minimum of three coats of clear waterborne acrylic urethane finish, sanding between coats with 220-grit sandpaper.

hinges will be attached to the top. **NOTE:** If you are using a block plane, do not push the blade past the corner, or it will split the edge of the plywood.

For pen and pencil storage, drill two ⁷⁄₁₆-inch-diameter holes and two ⁵⁄₁₆-inch-diameter holes in the 3x3½-inch pen and pencil holder shelf (see Fig. 4,

Wall File

WITH MORE PEOPLE working at home than ever before, the home office has become an important area in many apartments and houses. Those who bring work home from the office also are faced with the need to convert existing space into practical work and storage areas. One way to deal with this is by constructing this wall file, designed to hold 9¼x11¾-inch letter-size folders, 8½x11-inch legal pads and 4⅛x9½-inch business envelopes. The eight center cubbies can accommodate stationery, envelopes, incoming mail, bills and other papers. It is secured to the wall by screwing the back into the wall studs. We accented the clear birch plywood by painting the dividers a bright cadmium red before installing them.

MATERIALS LIST

Quantity	Size	Description	Location or Use
1	36x48 inches	¾-inch birch plywood	case (top, bottom & ends)
1	24x48 inches	½-inch birch plywood	partitions, shelf & back
1	33⅜x38⅛ inches	⅛-inch birch plywood	dividers
2	48-inch strips	¾-inch half-round molding	trim
2	14-inch strips	¾-inch half-round molding	trim
2	12½-inch strips	½-inch half-round molding	trim
1	15½-inch strip	½-inch half-round molding	trim
1 box	1½-inch	finish nails	case, partitions & shelf
1 box	1-inch	brads	trim
4	2½-inch	#10 roundhead screws with washers	
1 bottle	8 ounces	carpenter's glue	
1 sheet	60-grit	sandpaper	
1 sheet	120-grit	sandpaper	
1 sheet	220-grit	sandpaper	
1 can	10 ounces	water-based wood putty	
1 pint		paint or clear waterborne acrylic urethane wood finish	

Fig. 1

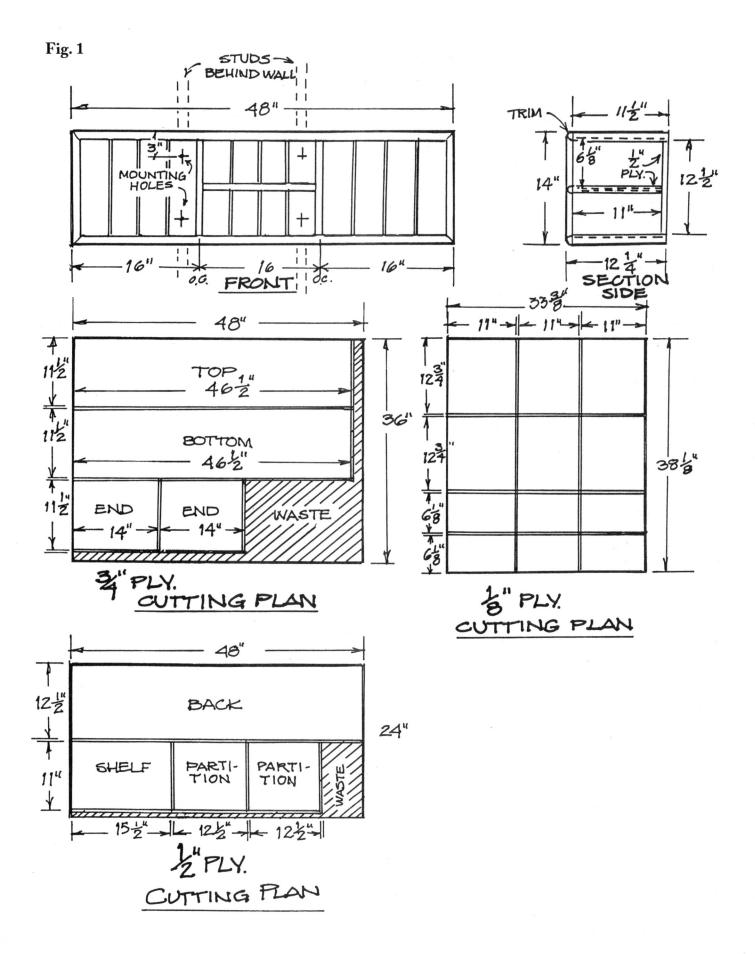

STUDS → BEHIND WALL

48"

3"

MOUNTING HOLES

16" 16 16"
O.C. **FRONT** O.C.

TRIM

11½"

6⅛"   ½" PLY.

14"   11"   12½"

12¼"

SECTION SIDE

48"

11½"   TOP 46½"

11½"   BOTTOM 46½"   36"

11½"   END 14"   END 14"   WASTE

¾" PLY. CUTTING PLAN

33⅜"

11" 11" 11"

12¾"

12¾"   38⅛"

6⅛"

6⅛"

⅛" PLY. CUTTING PLAN

48"

12½"   BACK

11"   SHELF   PARTI-TION   PARTI-TION   WASTE   24"

15½"   12½"   12½"

½" PLY. CUTTING PLAN

Fig. 2

Using the Cutting Plan as your guide (see Fig. 1), begin by cutting out the top, bottom and two end pieces for the case from the ¾-inch plywood. Next, cut out the two partitions, the middle shelf and the back pieces from ½-inch plywood.

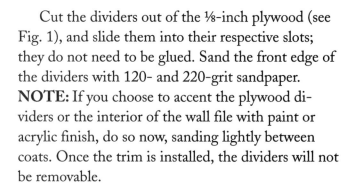

Before the case of the wall file is assembled, ⅛-inch-deep slots have to be cut in the top, bottom and shelf pieces to hold the dividers. Measure for the placement of the slots by dividing the length of the unit (48 inches) into thirds (16 inches). Then divide each third into four equal sections, making a total of 12 pigeonholes, and mark them on the underneath side of the top piece (see Fig. 2). **NOTE:** To divide a rectangle in half, draw lines from corner to corner and mark where they intersect.

After all the divider slots and locations for the partitions have been marked on the top piece, transfer these measurements to the bottom and the middle shelf pieces by laying all three boards down on the floor and drawing the lines across the boards using a T-square (see Fig. 2). **NOTE:** The middle shelf will have to be turned over and marked on the other side as well. Use a circular saw, table saw or radial arm saw with a ⅛-inch-wide blade to cut a ⅛ x ⅛-inch dado at the divider lines.

Assemble the case by gluing and nailing the ends to the top, bottom and back, using 1½-inch finish nails spaced 3 inches apart.

Glue and nail the two partitions and the middle shelf together, positioning the shelf halfway up the partition pieces (see Fig. 3). Slide this unit into the case at the partition locations previously made and glue and nail it from the top and bottom, placing nails every 3 inches.

Cut the dividers out of the ⅛-inch plywood (see Fig. 1), and slide them into their respective slots; they do not need to be glued. Sand the front edge of the dividers with 120- and 220-grit sandpaper. **NOTE:** If you choose to accent the plywood dividers or the interior of the wall file with paint or acrylic finish, do so now, sanding lightly between coats. Once the trim is installed, the dividers will not be removable.

The front edges of the case, partitions and shelf piece are trimmed with half-round molding. The purpose of the trim is to hide the ends of the ⅛-inch dadoes and to hold the dividers in place. Cut two 48-inch-long strips of ¾-inch half-round and two 14-inch-long strips of ¾-inch half-round. Miter the ends of each piece at a 45-degree angle, and glue and nail them onto the front edges of the case, using 1-inch brads. Cut the ½-inch half-round molding to size (see Materials List) and glue and nail it to the front of the two partitions and the center shelf piece. Set the nail heads, fill with wood putty and sand the outside of the completed unit, using 60-, 120- and 220-grit sandpaper.

To finish the outside of the wall file, apply at least three coats of either paint or a clear waterborne acrylic urethane finish, sanding lightly between coats with 220-grit sandpaper. We chose the second

Fig. 3

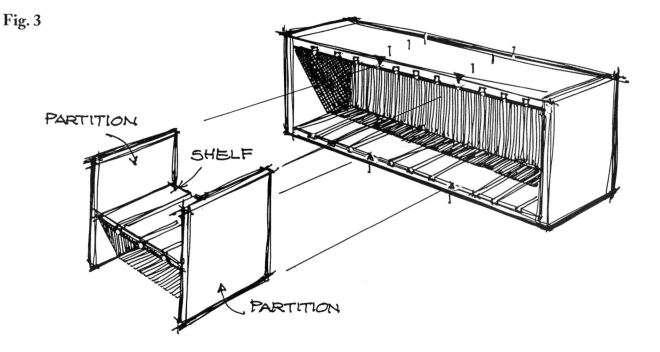

PARTITION

SHELF

PARTITION

option, giving our wall file a smooth, finished look that matched our apartment furniture.

To hang the unit on the wall, find and mark the stud locations behind the wall (see page 16, Attaching to the Wall). Drill two ³⁄₁₆-inch-diameter holes through the back of the unit, 3 inches below the top, the same distance apart as the studs. Determine how high you want your wall file to be, then drill a ⅛-inch-diameter hole in the wall 3 inches below this point. Screw the unit to the wall and interior stud, using a 2½-inch #10 roundhead screw and washer. Place a level on the top of the unit and drill another screw into the right hole. Since this unit will be rather heavy when filled, drill two more holes and insert screws lower down and into the same wall studs (see Fig. 1, Front View).

Desk Tray

ALTHOUGH PLASTIC DESK TRAYS are just as functional as wooden ones, they simply don't look as pleasing. This is a perfect opportunity to make use of that scrap of exotic wood that you've been saving in your shop. Substitute a piece of cherry, redwood, ash, cypress or other specialty wood for the clear pine specified below. No matter what wood you use, rabbeted corners are an absolute necessity for this project, since you'll want to place your handiwork in a highly visible spot.

Begin by rip-cutting the entire ½x4 pine board into a 2¼-inch-wide piece. Then cut that length into two 9¾-inch-long pieces for the front and back and two 12-inch-long pieces for the sides, as shown in the Cutting Plan (see Fig. 1). Rabbet both ends of the front and back pieces, ½ inch wide by ⅜ inch deep (see Fig. 2). Next, cut a ⅛x¼-inch dado ¼ inch from the bottom on the inside of all four pieces to accept the bottom of the box (see Fig. 3).

To make the scooped cut in the front piece, trace the outline of a small saucer or 1-gallon paint can (you need a 4-inch radius) onto the wood, 1 inch down from the top edge and approximately 5 inches wide (see Fig. 3, Front View). Cut out the shape, using an electric jigsaw, and sand it smooth, using 60-, 120- and 220-grit sandpaper.

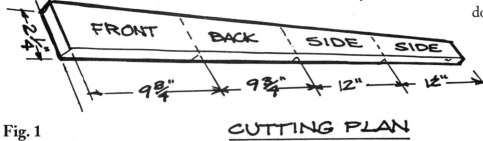

Fig. 1

CUTTING PLAN

MATERIALS LIST			
Quantity	**Size**	**Description**	**Location or Use**
1	48 inches	½x4 clear pine	sides, back & front
1	9¼ x 11¾ inches	⅛-inch birch plywood	bottom
1 bottle	8 ounces	carpenter's glue	
1 sheet	60-grit	sandpaper	
1 sheet	120-grit	sandpaper	
1 sheet	220-grit	sandpaper	
1 pint		clear waterborne acrylic urethane wood finish	

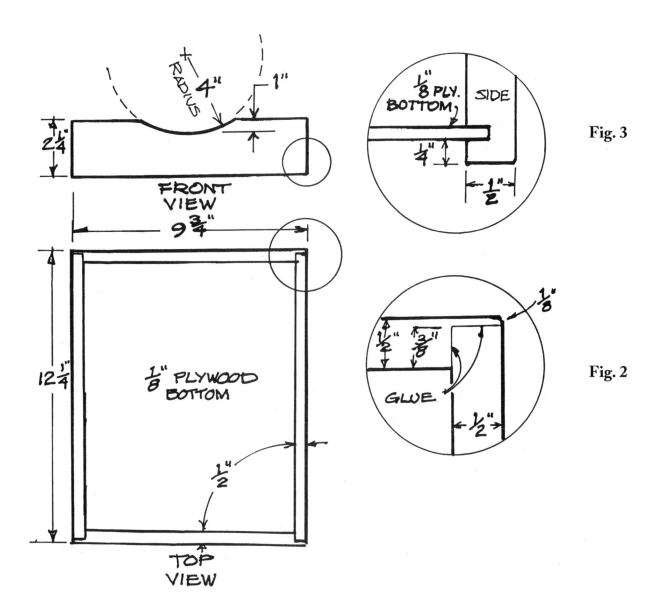

FRONT VIEW

TOP VIEW

Fig. 3

Fig. 2

Cut a piece of ⅛-inch plywood to measure 9¼ inches by 11¾ inches. Glue and fit it into the ⅛x¼-inch dado in the sides, back and front of the box. The sides should automatically fit into the rabbeted corners. Glue and clamp the pieces in place, allowing the glue to set up for several hours.

Sand all the surfaces of the box, using 60-, 120- and 120-grit sandpaper. Finish it with three coats of clear acrylic urethane, sanding with 220-grit sandpaper between coats.

Divided Pen & Pencil Box

THIS DESKTOP BOX makes a perfect organizer for all those loose pens and pencils that clutter your desk. It also looks decorative on any table or work surface. We made ours out of cypress because of its smooth grain and rich, warm color, but any exotic wood, such as teak, ash or walnut, will serve as well.

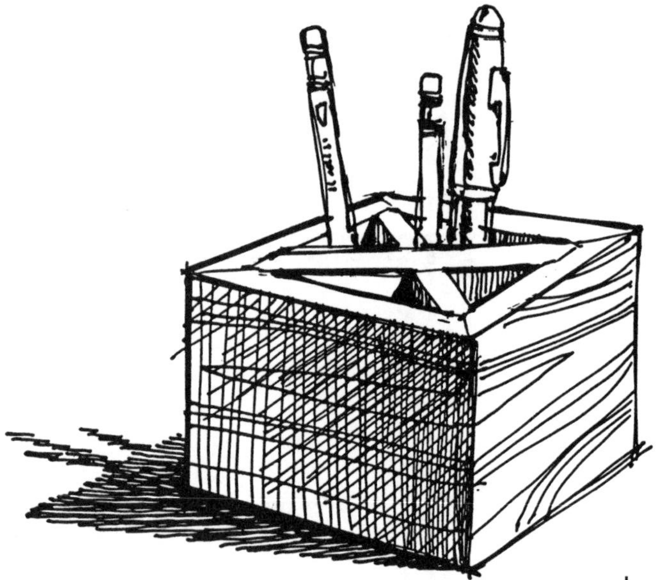

All the pieces for this project can be cut from a single 33¼-inch-long piece of 1x4 exotic wood (see Fig. 1), ripped to a thickness of ⅜ inch. To rip the board, set your table saw for a ⅜-inch-wide cut and run the board, on edge, through the saw blade. Use a

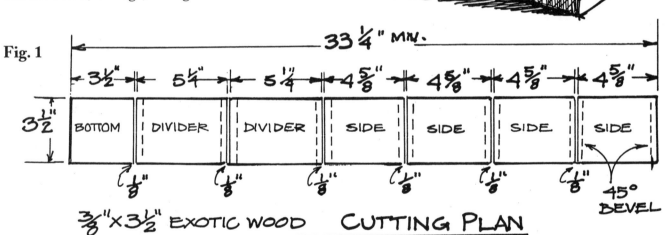

Fig. 1

33 ¼" MIN.

3½"   5¼"   5¼"   4⅝"   4⅝"   4⅝"   4⅝"

3½"

| BOTTOM | DIVIDER | DIVIDER | SIDE | SIDE | SIDE | SIDE |

⅛"   ⅛"   ⅛"   ⅛"   ⅛"   ⅛"

45° BEVEL

⅜" X 3½" EXOTIC WOOD   CUTTING PLAN

MATERIALS LIST

Quantity	Size	Description	Location or Use
4	3½ x 4⅝ inches	⅜-inch cypress	sides
2	3½ x 5¼ inches	⅜-inch cypress	diagonal dividers
1	3½ x 3½ inches	⅜-inch cypress	bottom
1 bottle	8 ounces	carpenter's glue	
1 sheet	60-grit	sandpaper	
1 sheet	120-grit	sandpaper	
1 sheet	220-grit	sandpaper	
1 pint		clear waterborne acrylic urethane wood finish	

Fig. 2

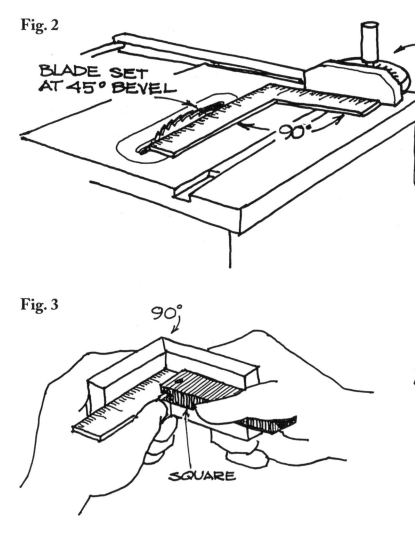

BLADE SET AT 45° BEVEL

MITER GAUGE

90°

Fig. 3

90°

SQUARE

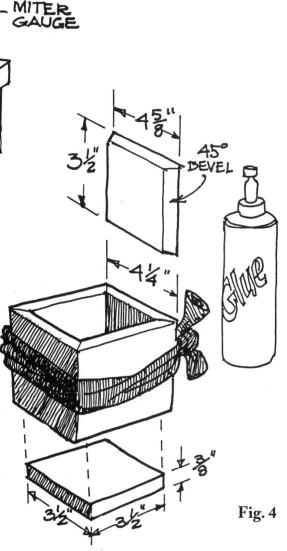

4⅝"

3½"

45° BEVEL

4¼"

Glue

⅜"

3½"

3½"

Fig. 4

"featherboard" (see pages 11 & 12, Section I) to keep the stock pressed against the fence. Turn the board over and repeat the same process on the other side. **TIP:** Spraying silicone on the board helps to make the blade slide through more easily.

The success of this project depends on your being able to make very accurate beveled cuts, so before beginning, check with a square to make sure that your miter gauge is set at a perfect 90-degree (right) angle to your saw blade and that the blade is at a 45-degree angle to the wood (see Fig. 2). Make a test cut by running a piece of scrap wood through the blade. Take the resulting two pieces of wood, turn one over, and fit the two angled ends together. They should form a 90-degree angle (see Fig. 3).

To make the sides of the box, cut four pieces,

each 4⅝ inches long, beveling each end at a 45-degree angle (see Fig. 4). Shave off the ends of each piece by making successive passes through the saw blade until each piece is exactly 4¼ inches long on its widest side. Stand the four pieces up together to make sure they are all the same length, trimming them if necessary.

Glue the four sides of the box together, placing a thin bead of carpenter's glue on each beveled end. While the glue is drying, hold the sides together either with a rubber band or a piece of bicycle inner tube (see Fig. 4).

Cut the ⅜x3½x3½-inch bottom piece and glue it into the base of the box.

Divided Pen & Pencil Box

Fig. 5

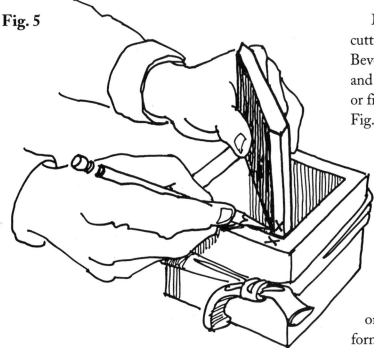

Make the two diagonal inserts for the box by cutting two pieces, each 3½ inches by 5¼ inches. Bevel each side of each end at a 45-degree angle and shave the angles down until the piece measures or fits perfectly on a diagonal inside the box (see Fig. 5). Do the same for the second piece. Label the edges so you can put the pieces back together in the correct order.

Because of the thickness of the bottom piece, the diagonal inserts extend beyond the top of the box. To remedy this, mark and cut off the excess wood so that the inserts are flush with the top of the box. When each piece fits perfectly, place one piece in the box on the diagonal and hold the other piece above it, forming an X. Mark where they intersect (see Fig. 6) and using an electric jigsaw with a scroll saw blade, cut ⅜-inch-wide notches, 1½ inches long, in the center of each piece.

Fig. 6

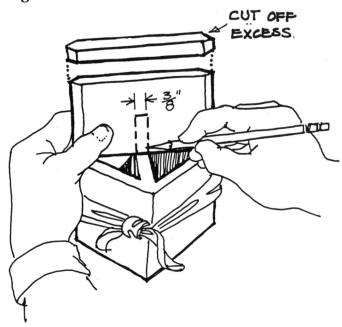

CUT OFF EXCESS.

⅜"

Join the two pieces together to make an X, and glue and fit them inside the box. Sand the entire box with 60-, 120- and 220-grit sandpaper. Finish with three coats of a clear waterborne acrylic urethane, sanding lightly between each coat with 220-grit sandpaper.

Wrapping & Mailing Center

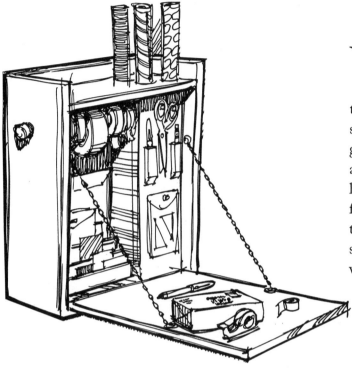

WHETHER YOU ARE wrapping a gift or mailing a manuscript, this compact cabinet holds all the essentials, from scissors and tape to stamps and string. All are tucked away out of sight and neatly arranged so they can be found at a glance. The dowel displays ribbons, twine and tape and provides a convenient means to cut off measured lengths. Four holes in the top keep rolls of paper from being dented or misplaced, and dividers inside the wrapping center hold envelopes, labels and stamps. The fold-out front piece creates a convenient work surface for wrapping and addressing packages.

When the front is closed, the unit turns back into an attractive wall cabinet, blending in with the interior of your room.

MATERIALS LIST

Quantity	Size	Description	Location or Use
1	28x51 inches	½-inch birch plywood	back, top, fronts, bottom, sides & envelope base
1	9x22 inches	⅛-inch birch plywood	envelope holder dividers
1	11 inches	1-inch-diameter dowel	tape & ribbon rack
2	1-inch	⅜-inch-diameter wood pegs	scissors supports
2	12 inches	⅛-inch chain	fold-out front
1		magnetic catch	fold-out front
1	15¼ inches	½x½-inch continuous (piano) hinge with screws	fold-out front
1 box	1⅛-inch	wire nails	compartment
1	¾-inch	brass brad	
2	½-inch	#4 roundhead screws & washers	
1 bottle	8 ounces	carpenter's glue	
1 sheet	60-grit	sandpaper	
1 sheet	120-grit	sandpaper	
1 sheet	220-grit	sandpaper	
1 pint		semigloss paint or clear waterborne acrylic urethane wood finish	

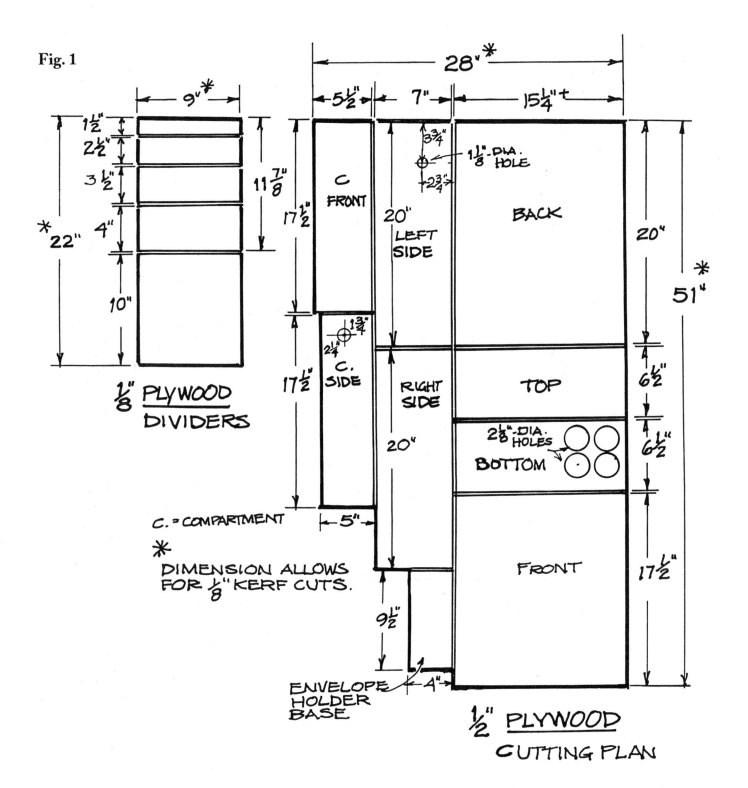

Fig. 1

9" *

1½"
2½"
3½"
4"
10"

22" *

11⅞"

½" PLYWOOD DIVIDERS

28" *

5½" · 7" · 15¼"†

C FRONT
17½"

C. SIDE
17½"

20"
LEFT SIDE

RIGHT SIDE
20"

3¾"
1⅛"-DIA. HOLE
2¾"

BACK

20"

TOP

2⅛"-DIA. HOLES
BOTTOM

6½"
6½"

FRONT
17½"

1¾"
2¼"

5"

C. = COMPARTMENT

* DIMENSION ALLOWS FOR ⅛" KERF CUTS.

51" *

9½"

ENVELOPE HOLDER BASE

4"

½" PLYWOOD CUTTING PLAN

Begin by cutting out all the pieces, using the measurements shown on the Cutting Plan (see Fig. 1). The back, front, bottom, sides and top (plus the base of the envelope holder) are all cut from one 28x51-inch piece of ½-inch plywood. The envelope holder dividers are all cut from one 9x22-inch piece of ⅛-inch plywood. To avoid confusion later, label all the pieces on the edge of the wood. Check to make sure that the top and bottom pieces are exactly the same lengths.

With a standard hole saw (used for drilling out holes in door locksets), cut the four 2⅛-inch-diameter holes in the top piece (see Fig. 2). To locate the center points for the drill, see Fig. 3 (Enlarged Top Detail).

Fig. 3

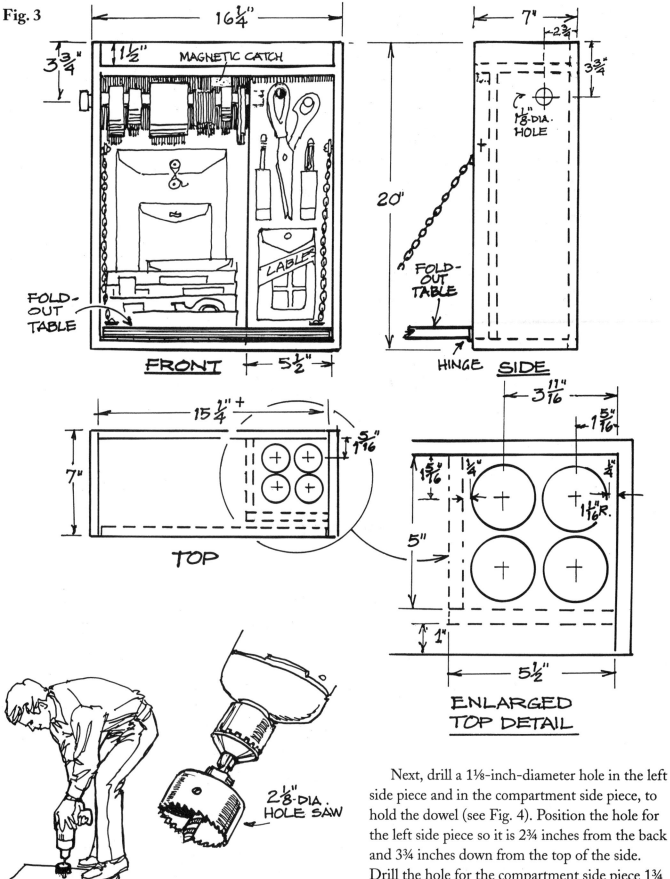

16¼"

1½" MAGNETIC CATCH

3¾"

FOLD-OUT TABLE

FRONT

5½"

7"

2¾"

3¾"

1⅛"-DIA. HOLE

20"

FOLD-OUT TABLE

HINGE   SIDE

15¼" +

1⁵⁄₁₆"

7"

TOP

3¹¹⁄₁₆"

1⁵⁄₁₆"

1⁵⁄₁₆"   ¼"   ¼"   1¹⁄₁₆"R.

5"

1"

5½"

ENLARGED TOP DETAIL

2⅛"-DIA. HOLE SAW

Fig. 2

Next, drill a 1⅛-inch-diameter hole in the left side piece and in the compartment side piece, to hold the dowel (see Fig. 4). Position the hole for the left side piece so it is 2¾ inches from the back and 3¾ inches down from the top of the side. Drill the hole for the compartment side piece 1¾ inches down from the top and 2¼ inches in from the back of the piece. To avoid tear-out when drilling the holes, drill only partway through, until the point of the drill shows through the other side. Turn the board over and complete the holes, drilling from the other side.

Sand all the plywood surfaces that will face inside the unit, using 60-, 120- and 220-grit sandpaper.

Lay the back piece on your work table and draw a line 5½ inches in from the right side, where the compartment piece will be positioned (see Fig. 4). Glue the compartment side piece in place, 2 inches below the top edge of the back. Glue the top, bottom and sides together. When the glue has set up, nail all the pieces together, using 1⅛-inch wire nails, spaced approximately 2 inches apart. Then glue the front of the compartment in place.

To build the ribbon and tape holder, cut a 1-inch-diameter dowel 11 inches long. Measure in 3⁄16 inch from one end and make a mark. Measure in and

make a second mark ½ inch in from the first mark (see Fig. 5). Set the fence on your table saw 3⁄16 inch from the blade and ⅛ inch up from the surface of the work table. Rest the dowel against your miter gauge and carefully roll the dowel into the blade until you have cut a ½-inch-wide shoulder in the dowel (see Fig. 6). Round off the end edges with sandpaper, then slip the dowel through the two 1⅛-inch-diameter holes. Sand all the exposed surfaces, using 60-, 120- and 220-grit sandpaper.

To make the envelope holder, cut three dadoes, each ⅛ inch wide and ¼ inch deep, in the ½-inch-plywood base piece (see Fig. 7). Sand the edges of the five dividers, and glue the three middle ones into the base and the first and last ones to the front and back edges of the plywood base (see Fig. 8).

To make the pen and pencil holders, drill two holes, one 9⁄32 inch in diameter for the pencil and one ⅜ inch in diameter for the pen, in the end of a piece of scrap ¾-inch-thick board (see Fig. 9). Rip-cut two pieces of the board into ½ x ¾-inch strips, 3 inches long, and bevel the bottom ends to a 45-degree angle (see Fig. 10).

Lay out your scissors, box of labels, and pen and pencil holders on the front of the compartment and mark where they should be positioned. Glue the pen and pencil

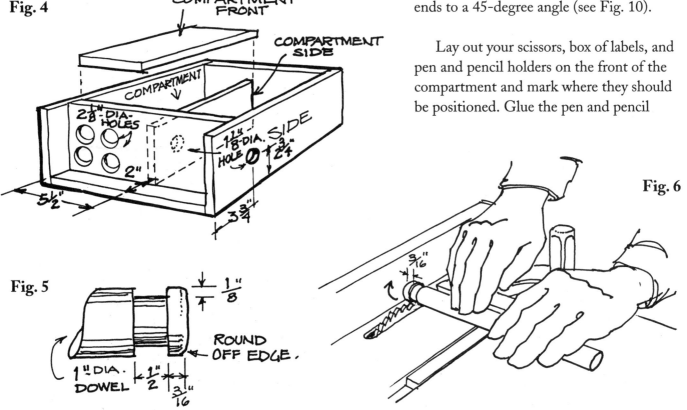

Fig. 4

Fig. 5

Fig. 6

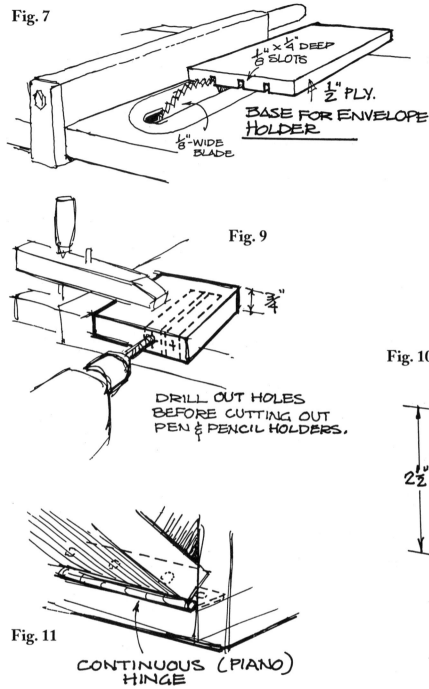

Fig. 7

$\frac{1}{8}" \times \frac{1}{4}"$ DEEP SLOTS

$\frac{1}{2}"$ PLY.

BASE FOR ENVELOPE HOLDER

$\frac{1}{8}"$-WIDE BLADE

Fig. 9

$\frac{3}{4}"$

DRILL OUT HOLES BEFORE CUTTING OUT PEN & PENCIL HOLDERS.

Fig. 11

CONTINUOUS (PIANO) HINGE

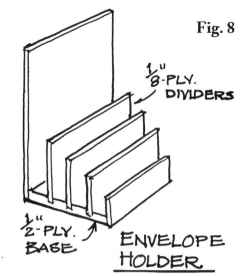

Fig. 8

$\frac{1}{8}"$-PLY. DIVIDERS

$\frac{1}{2}"$-PLY. BASE

ENVELOPE HOLDER

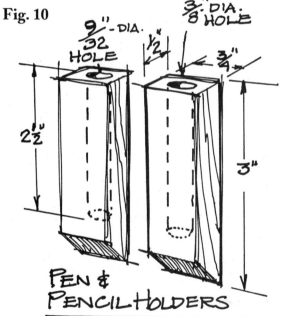

Fig. 10

$\frac{9}{32}"$-DIA. HOLE

$\frac{3}{8}"$-DIA. HOLE

$\frac{1}{2}"$

$\frac{3}{4}"$

$2\frac{1}{2}"$

$3"$

PEN & PENCIL HOLDERS

holders in place and hammer in a ¾-inch brass brad to hold the label box. Drill two holes for the ⅜-inch-diameter wood pegs on which the scissors will hang, then glue and insert the pegs.

Test-fit the fold-out front piece to make sure that it fits neatly between the sides, top and bottom of the unit. Screw a 15¼-inch-long continuous (piano) hinge along the bottom edge of the fold-out front and the inside edge of the cabinet (see Fig. 11).

Install a magnetic catch centered underneath the top piece and on the fold-out front. With the fold-out front opened, mark where the two 12-inch-long chains should go and attach them using ½-inch #4 screws and washers at each end.

The mailing center can either be painted with two coats of semigloss paint or finished with three coats of a clear waterborne acrylic urethane finish.

Storage Stool or Ottoman

ORGANIZATION OF STORAGE space is especially important in a home office. Because of the many built-in distractions that go along with working at home, it is often difficult to separate one's personal life from one's professional life. Office files and work projects should be "camouflaged" so when the workday ends, they blend in with the surrounding environment. This storage stool/ottoman combination is a perfect way to put the lid down on work at the end of the day.

Although we have included A-A plywood in the Materials List, bass, birch or teak plywood will also work well for this project. We covered the foam rubber on top of our ottoman with a rich burgundy velveteen, which gives the stool a finished look that fits in equally well in the living room, office or bedroom. Nylon casters enable it to be moved easily from room to room. The stool contains a drawer, a small yet accessible file cabinet and a shelf/compartment in which to store telephone directories, a dictionary or other reference books. When it is not being used to sit or rest your feet on, the foam cushion, which is attached to a hinged top piece, flips up, revealing a flat work surface.

Begin by cutting all the pieces from the 48-inch-long 1x6 clear mahogany and the ½-inch plywood, using the Cutting Plan as your guide (see Fig. 1A & 1B). For the legs, rip four 1½x12-inch pieces, two 1x12-inch pieces and two ½x12-inch pieces. For the side trim, rip two pieces, each measuring 1½x14¾ inches; for the back trim, rip one piece, measuring 1½x14¼ inches.

Fig. 1A

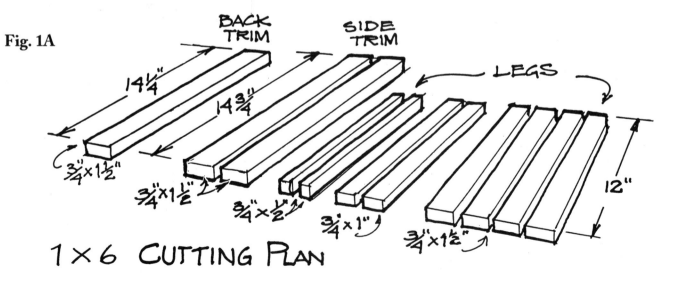

BACK TRIM SIDE TRIM LEGS

14¼" 14¾" 12"

¾"x1½" ¾"x1½" ¾"x1½" ¾"x1" ¾"x1½"

1×6 CUTTING PLAN

MATERIALS LIST

Quantity	Size	Description	Location or Use
1 sheet	4x4 feet	½-inch A-A plywood	front, back, sides, tops, bottom, divider & drawer
1	9½x13⅝ inches	⅛-inch birch plywood	drawer bottom
1	48 inches	1x6 clear Philippine mahogany	legs & trim pieces
1	9½ inches	1x4 hardwood	ledge
6	10 inches	½x¾-inch hardwood	drawer slide cleats & runners
1 pair	1x2-inch	brass hinges	bottom shelf
1	3-inch	touch latch	lower cabinet door
1	17½ inches	½x½-inch continuous (piano) hinge w/screws	top hinge
1	17½x17½ inches	1½-inch-thick foam	seat
1	27x27 inches	fabric	seat
1 pair	12-inch	Stanley brass-plated lid support	top
4	1⅝-inch-dia.	nylon twin-wheel plate casters	bottom
1 box	1½-inch	galvanized finish nails	drawer
6	¾-inch	#6 flathead screws	runners
8	1-inch	#6 flathead screws	seat
1 bottle	8 ounces	carpenter's glue	
1 can	10 ounces	water-based wood putty	
1 sheet	60-grit	sandpaper	
1 sheet	120-grit	sandpaper	
1 sheet	220-grit	sandpaper	
1 quart		clear waterborne acrylic urethane wood finish	

Fig. 1B

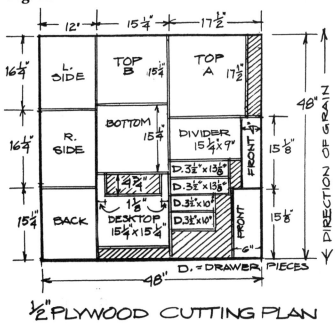

½" PLYWOOD CUTTING PLAN

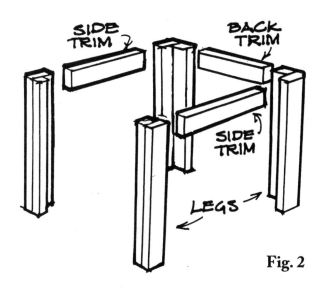

Fig. 2

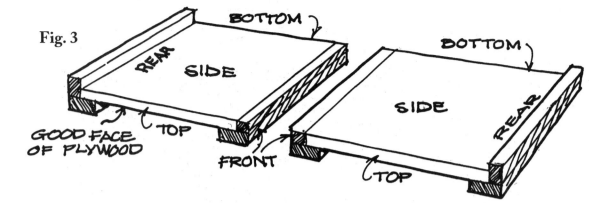

Fig. 3

BOTTOM

REAR

SIDE

TOP

GOOD FACE
OF PLYWOOD

FRONT

BOTTOM

SIDE

REAR

TOP

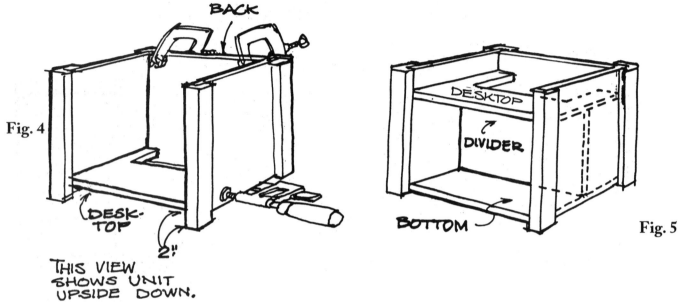

BACK

Fig. 4

DESK-
TOP

2"

THIS VIEW
SHOWS UNIT
UPSIDE DOWN.

DESKTOP

DIVIDER

BOTTOM

Fig. 5

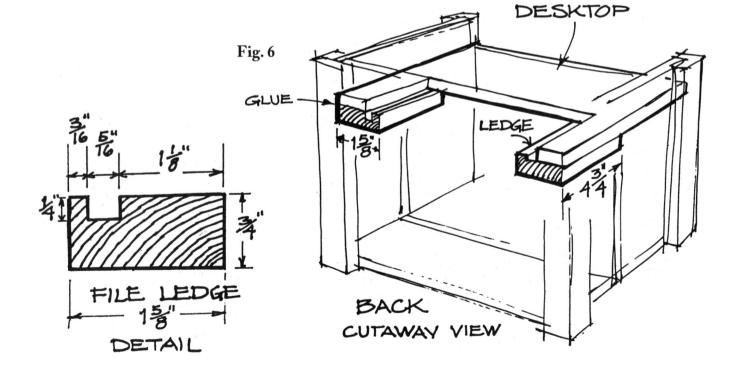

DESKTOP

Fig. 6

GLUE

LEDGE

1 5/8"

3/4"

$\frac{3}{16}$" $\frac{5}{16}$" $1\frac{1}{8}$"

$\frac{1}{4}$"

$\frac{3}{4}$"

FILE LEDGE

$1\frac{5}{8}$"

DETAIL

BACK
CUTAWAY VIEW

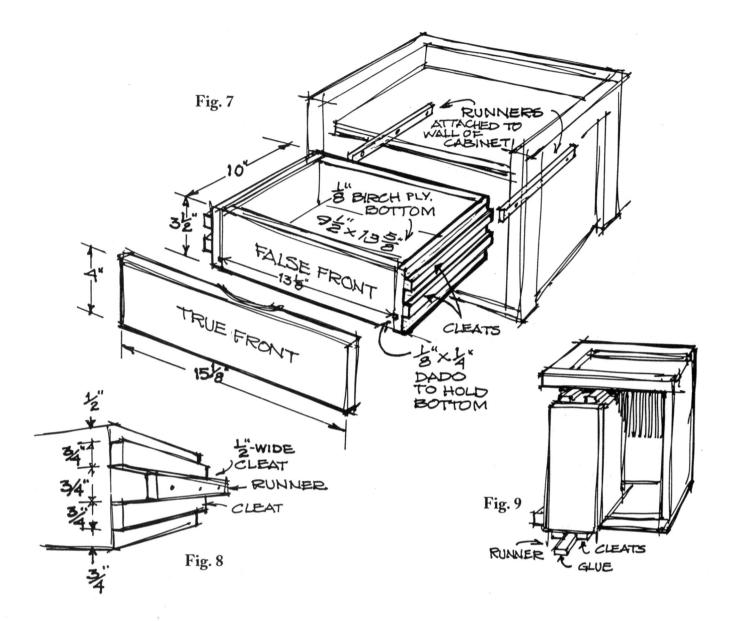

Fig. 7

RUNNERS ATTACHED TO WALL OF CABINET!

$\frac{1}{8}$" BIRCH PLY. BOTTOM
$9\frac{1}{2}$" × $13\frac{5}{8}$"

10"

$3\frac{1}{2}$"

FALSE FRONT
$13\frac{5}{8}$"

4"

TRUE FRONT

$15\frac{5}{8}$"

CLEATS

$\frac{1}{8}$" × $\frac{1}{4}$" DADO TO HOLD BOTTOM

$\frac{1}{2}$"

$\frac{3}{4}$"

$3\frac{3}{4}$"

$\frac{3}{4}$"

$\frac{1}{2}$"-WIDE CLEAT
RUNNER
CLEAT

Fig. 8

$\frac{3}{4}$"

Fig. 9

RUNNER   CLEATS
GLUE

Glue and clamp each leg together to form four L-shaped legs (see Fig. 2). **NOTE:** The two front legs are assembled in a different manner than the two back legs (see Fig. 10, Top View Detail). When the glue has dried, sand the legs so they are perfectly smooth, using 60-, 120- and 220-grit sandpaper.

Glue the two side panels to the two pairs of legs (see Fig. 3). **NOTE:** Make sure you have the pieces matched properly and that the good side of the plywood faces out. When the glue has dried completely (three to four hours), glue and clamp the back and the desktop pieces to the two side pieces, positioning the desktop 2 inches below the top edge of the panels (see Fig. 4). Then glue the bottom and the divider in place (see Fig. 5). The resulting file compartment will be 4¾ inches front to back.

To build a ledge on which to hang files, rip a 9½-inch-long piece of 1x4 hardwood so that it measures 1⅝ inches wide. Then cut it into two pieces, each 4¾ inches long. Cut a ⁵⁄₁₆-inch-wide dado, ¼ inch deep, ³⁄₁₆ inch from the edge of each piece (see Fig. 6, File Ledge Detail). Glue and clamp each piece to the underside of the two projecting arms of the desktop (see Fig. 6).

Glue and clamp the two side trim pieces and the back trim piece in place.

Fig. 10

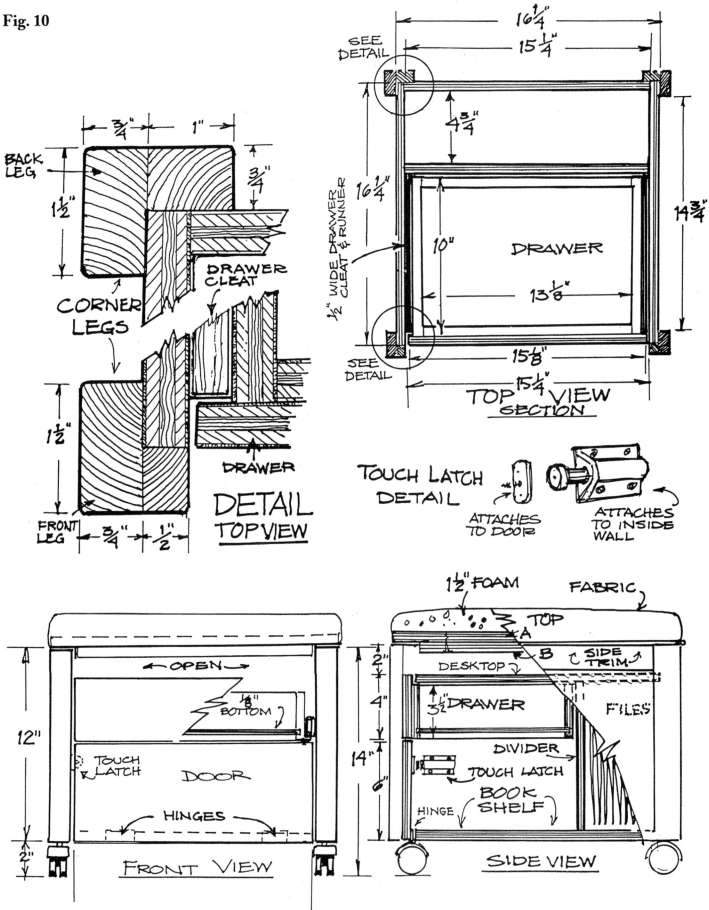

BACK LEG

CORNER LEGS

FRONT LEG

DRAWER CLEAT

DRAWER

DETAIL TOP VIEW

SEE DETAIL

½" WIDE DRAWER CLEAT & RUNNER

DRAWER

SEE DETAIL

TOP VIEW SECTION

TOUCH LATCH DETAIL

ATTACHES TO DOOR

ATTACHES TO INSIDE WALL

OPEN

BOTTOM

TOUCH LATCH

DOOR

HINGES

FRONT VIEW

1½" FOAM

FABRIC

TOP

DESKTOP

SIDE TRIM

DRAWER

FILES

DIVIDER

TOUCH LATCH

BOOK SHELF

HINGE

SIDE VIEW

Fig. 11

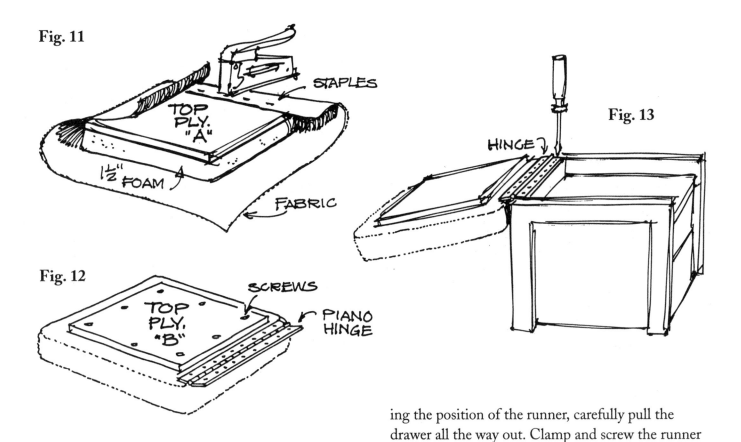

Fig. 12

Fig. 13

Construct a drawer to fit under the desktop. Begin by cutting a ⅛-inch-wide, ¼-inch-deep dado ¼ inch in from the bottom edge of all four drawer pieces (see Fig. 7). Cut a 9½x13⅝-inch piece of ⅛-inch birch plywood for the drawer bottom, and insert it into the dado in the sides, false front and back piece. Glue and nail the side pieces to the false front and back pieces, using 1½-inch galvanized finish nails (see Fig. 7). **NOTE:** The "true" front piece will be added later.

To mount the drawer to the box, rip six pieces of hardwood (poplar, birch, etc.), each ½x¾x10 inches long. Sand the pieces until smooth, using 220-grit sandpaper. Glue and clamp two parallel "cleats" to each side of the drawer, ¾ inch apart and ½ inch down from the top edge of the drawer (see Fig. 8). Test to make sure that the ¾-inch runner piece slides smoothly between the two cleats. Apply glue to one side of one of the runners, and turn the box on its side. Place the runner between the cleats so that the glued side is facing out, and carefully position the drawer in place (see Fig. 9). Allow the glue on the runner to set up for a few minutes. Without disturb-

ing the position of the runner, carefully pull the drawer all the way out. Clamp and screw the runner to the inside of the box, using ¾-inch countersunk flathead screws. Follow the same procedure for the other side of the unit.

Once the drawer is installed, glue and clamp the 4x15⅛-inch true front of the drawer onto the false front. This will allow you to make any necessary adjustments so that the front is aligned perfectly.

To make the bottom storage compartment, attach two 1x2-inch brass hinges to the front edge of the bottom shelf and the bottom inside face of the door (see Fig. 10, Front View). To hold the door shut, install a touch latch (see Fig. 10, Touch Latch Detail and Side View) on the left side of the door and on the inside of the box.

Cut a 17½x17½-inch piece of 1½-inch-thick foam and a 27x27-inch piece of fabric. Wrap the fabric around the foam and under the top (A) piece of ½-inch plywood. Fold in the corners neatly and staple the fabric to the plywood (see Fig. 11). Screw the second top (B) to the first top (A), using 1-inch countersunk #6 flathead screws (see Fig. 12).

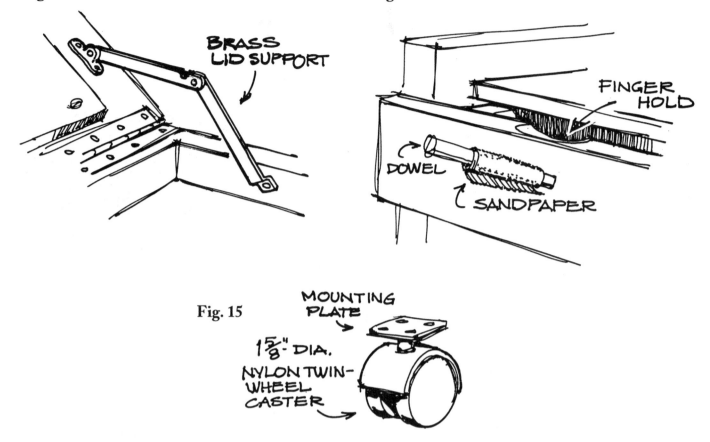

Fig. 14

BRASS LID SUPPORT

Fig. 16

FINGER HOLD

DOWEL

SANDPAPER

Fig. 15

MOUNTING PLATE

1⅝" DIA. NYLON TWIN-WHEEL CASTER

Cut and attach a ½ x ½ x 17½-inch continuous (piano) hinge to one of the bottom edges of the cushion/top. Screw the other side of the hinge to the top of the back trim (see Fig. 13).

To prevent the top lid from opening up too far, install a pair of Stanley brass-plated lid supports (see Sources), screwed to the lid and to the 2-inch-high sides above the desktop (see Fig. 14).

Attach four 1⅝-inch-diameter nylon twin-wheel casters (see Fig. 15), equipped with mounting plates and screws (see Sources). Screw one caster to the underneath side of each corner (see Fig. 10, Front & Side Views).

No hardware is necessary for the drawer; instead of installing a drawer pull, you can make a finger hold. Use a dowel wrapped with 60-grit sandpaper to shape the top inside edge of the drawer (see Fig. 16).

Fill any nail holes with wood putty and sand all the surfaces with 60-, 120- and 220-grit sandpaper. Finish with three coats of a clear waterborne acrylic urethane wood finish.

CD Holder

ALTHOUGH THERE ARE several sizes and shapes of CD holders available on the market today, this wedge-shaped container has the advantage of holding the CDs at an angle, which makes them easier to read and remove. It holds 36 single CDs, and the plywood dividers can easily be slipped out to accommodate double CDs. This project can be stained to match your furniture or, to protect it from fingerprints and show off the birch veneer, covered with a clear waterborne acrylic urethane finish.

Cut the two sides, the bottom front, the top/back and the inside back from the ½-inch birch plywood, following the Cutting Plan (see Fig. 1).

Using a table saw, bevel the bottom edges of the bottom front and the top pieces at a 45-degree angle (see Fig. 2).

Cut the slots that hold the ⅛-inch plywood dividers, using a ⅛-inch-wide saw blade on a radial arm saw. Do this by taping the top and the bottom front pieces together and running the saw blade through both pieces at the same time (see Fig. 3). Make a pencil mark on the saw fence, ⅝ inch away from the center of the saw blade, and use this mark as a reference point each time you move the board over to cut a slot. **NOTE:** In order for the top/back and bottom front to overlap the sides, you'll need to leave ½ inch on each end *before* measuring for the ⅝-inch on-center divider spacing.

Glue and clamp the top and side pieces together, then glue the inside back piece in place, so that it is 4½ inches from the front of the unit (see Fig. 4,

MATERIALS LIST

Quantity	Size	Description	Location or Use
1	23½ x 25⅞ inches	½-inch birch plywood	bottom front, top, inside back & sides
35	4½ x 5¼ inches	⅛-inch birch plywood	dividers
1	60 inches	⅛ x ½-inch birch	trim (optional)
1 bottle	8 ounces	carpenter's glue	
1 sheet	60-grit	sandpaper	
1 sheet	220-grit	sandpaper	
1 pint		clear waterborne acrylic urethane finish	

Fig. 1

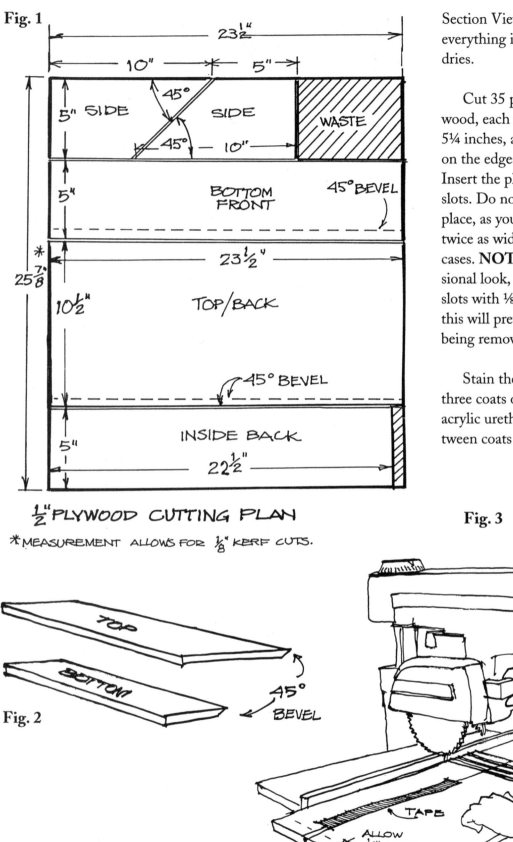

23½"

10" — 5"

45°
5" SIDE — SIDE — WASTE
45° — 10"

5" — BOTTOM FRONT — 45° BEVEL

*
25⅞"
7.°

10½" — TOP/BACK

45° BEVEL

5" — INSIDE BACK
22½"

½" PLYWOOD CUTTING PLAN

*MEASUREMENT ALLOWS FOR ⅛" KERF CUTS.

Fig. 2

TOP

BOTTOM

45° BEVEL

Fig. 3

ALLOW ½" SPACE AT EACH END.

TAPE

CUT ⅛" X ⅛" DADOES ⅝" APART O.C.

Section View). Check to make sure everything is square before the glue dries.

Cut 35 pieces of ⅛-inch birch plywood, each measuring 4½ inches by 5¼ inches, and sand off any burrs left on the edges, using 60-grit sandpaper. Insert the plywood dividers into the slots. Do not glue the dividers in place, as you may need a few openings twice as wide, to hold double CD cases. **NOTE:** For a more professional look, cover the top of the dado slots with ⅛x½-inch trim; however, this will prevent the dividers from being removable.

Stain the unit or cover it with three coats of a clear waterborne acrylic urethane finish, sanding between coats with 220-grit sandpaper.

Fig. 4

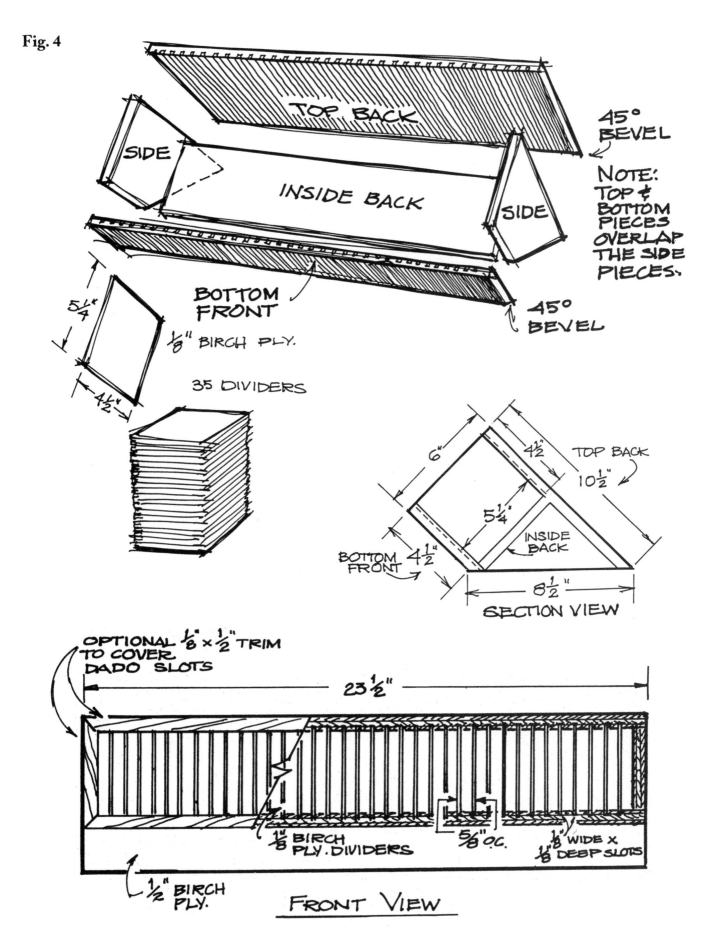

TOP BACK

45° BEVEL

SIDE

INSIDE BACK

SIDE

NOTE: TOP & BOTTOM PIECES OVERLAP THE SIDE PIECES.

$5\frac{1}{4}$"

BOTTOM FRONT

45° BEVEL

$\frac{1}{8}$" BIRCH PLY.

$4\frac{1}{2}$"

35 DIVIDERS

6"

$4\frac{1}{2}$"

TOP BACK

$10\frac{1}{2}$"

$5\frac{1}{4}$"

INSIDE BACK

BOTTOM FRONT

$4\frac{1}{2}$"

$8\frac{1}{2}$"

SECTION VIEW

OPTIONAL $\frac{1}{8}$" × $\frac{1}{2}$" TRIM TO COVER DADO SLOTS

$23\frac{1}{2}$"

$\frac{1}{8}$" BIRCH PLY. DIVIDERS

$\frac{5}{8}$" O.C.

$\frac{1}{8}$" WIDE × $\frac{1}{8}$" DEEP SLOTS

$\frac{1}{2}$" BIRCH PLY.

FRONT VIEW

VCR Storage Unit

A N ATTRACTIVE PIECE OF FURNITURE for almost any room, this unit has enough compartments to neatly store a VCR, videotapes and a video camera, and it's sturdy enough to support a TV on top. The spacious top shelf has an open back for ventilation and allows extra space for the possibility of upsizing your present VCR. The center drawer slides out easily on nylon rollers and holds 22 videotapes. The touch-latched bottom compartment is big enough to hold a video camera and a power bar and to hide all the unsightly electrical cords that otherwise crisscross each other on the floor.

Cut out all the pieces, using the measurements shown on the Cutting Plan as your guide (see Fig. 1). Use a table saw to cut a ⅝x¾-inch rabbet out of the ends of the top piece to accept the ¾-inch plywood side pieces (see Fig. 2 & Rabbet Joint Detail).

Mark the position of the shelves by laying the

MATERIALS LIST

Quantity	Size	Description	Location or Use
1 sheet	4x8 feet	¾-inch birch, bass or luane plywood	sides, top, shelves, fronts
1	18⅜x34⅛ inches	¼-inch plywood	back, drawer bottom
1	8 feet	½x4 clear pine	drawer
1 pair	14-inch	white Grass #6650 bottom-mounted glide roller drawer slides	
1 pair	1½x2-inch	butt hinges	
1	3-inch	touch latch	
1 box	1¼-inch	annular panel nails	
1 can	10 ounces	water-based wood putty	
1 bottle	8 ounces	carpenter's glue	
1 sheet	120-grit	sandpaper	
1 sheet	220-grit	sandpaper	
1 quart		clear waterborne acrylic urethane finish	

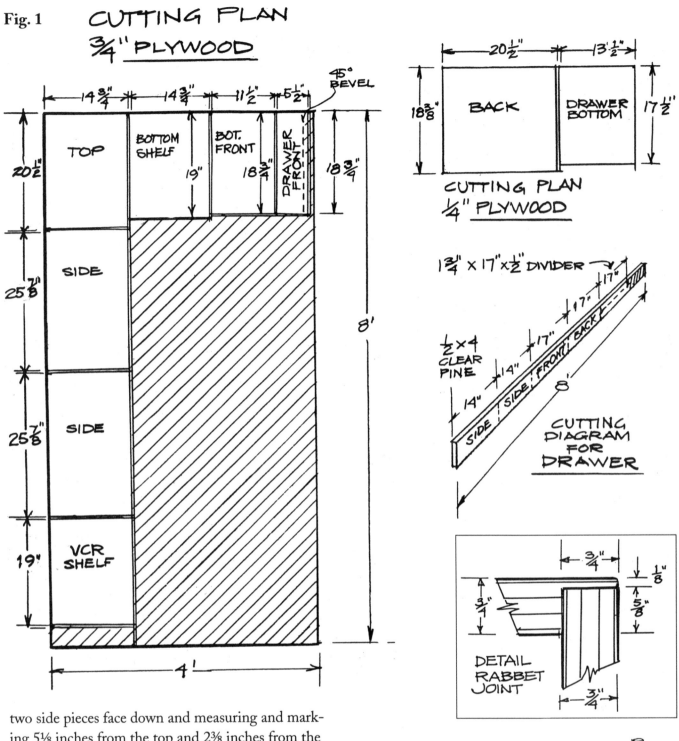

Fig. 1 CUTTING PLAN ¾" PLYWOOD

TOP

BOTTOM SHELF

BOT. FRONT

DRAWER FRONT

SIDE

SIDE

VCR SHELF

14¾"   14¾"   11½"   5½"   45° BEVEL

20½"   25⅞"   25⅞"   19"

19"   18¾"   18¾"

4'   8'

CUTTING PLAN ¼" PLYWOOD

BACK   DRAWER BOTTOM

20½"   13½"   18⅜"   17½"

1¾" × 17" × ½" DIVIDER

½×4 CLEAR PINE

14"   14"   17"   17"   17"

SIDE | SIDE | FRONT | BACK

8'

CUTTING DIAGRAM FOR DRAWER

DETAIL RABBET JOINT

¾"   ⅛"   ⅝"   ¾"   ¾"

two side pieces face down and measuring and marking 5⅛ inches from the top and 2⅜ inches from the bottom of each (see Fig. 3). Draw two parallel lines ¾ inch apart across both side pieces to show where the two shelves will be located.

Before attaching the back piece to the side pieces, make a temporary back stop by screwing a 2x4 block to your workbench. Position the left side piece against the block and glue and nail the ¼-inch ply-

Fig. 2

Fig. 3

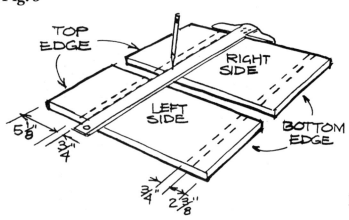

TOP EDGE

RIGHT SIDE

LEFT SIDE

BOTTOM EDGE

5 1/8"

3/4"

3/4" 2 3/8"

Fig. 4

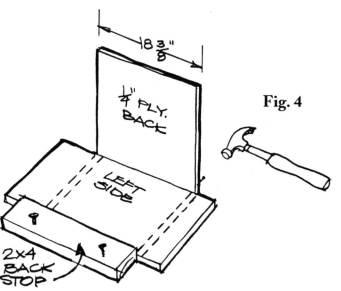

18 3/8"

1/4" PLY. BACK

LEFT SIDE

2x4 BACK STOP

Fig. 5

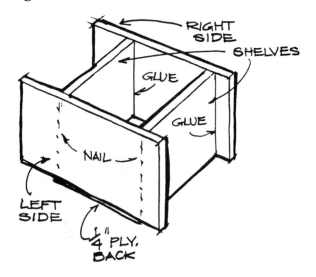

RIGHT SIDE

SHELVES

GLUE

GLUE

NAIL

LEFT SIDE

1/4" PLY. BACK

Fig. 6

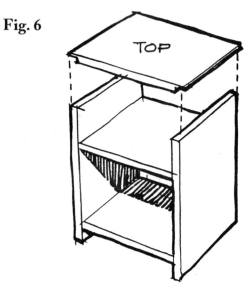

TOP

DRAWER SLIDE

FALSE FRONT

TRUE FRONT

1/4 x 1/4" DADO

Fig. 7

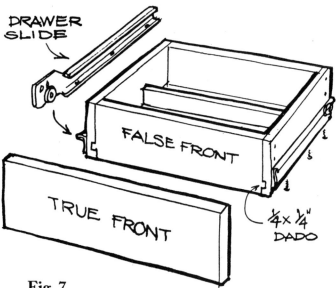

wood back piece to the back edge of the left side piece, using 1¼-inch annular panel nails, spaced every 3 inches (see Fig. 4). Turn the unit around, so that the right side piece is braced against the 2x4 back stop, and nail the back piece to the right side piece in the same manner.

Turn the assembly over on its back, and position the top and bottom shelves in place by flexing (bending) the sides of the unit out, then placing a bead of

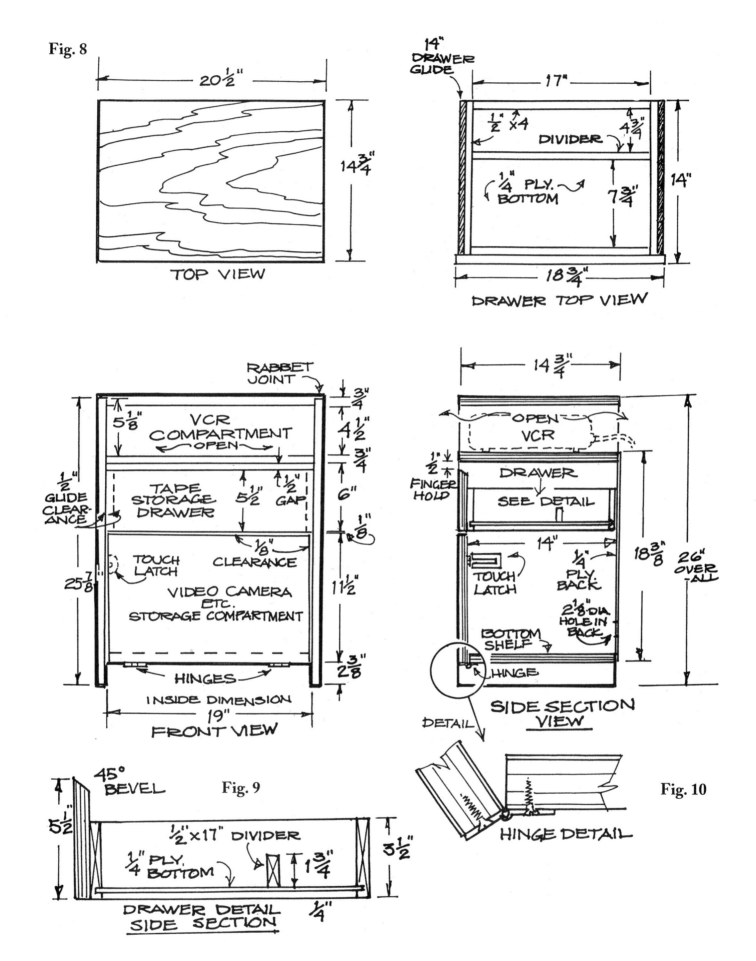

Fig. 8

20½"

14¾"

TOP VIEW

14" DRAWER GUIDE

17"

½" ×4

DIVIDER

4¾"

¼ PLY. BOTTOM

7¾"

14"

18¾"

DRAWER TOP VIEW

RABBET JOINT

¾"

5⅛"

VCR COMPARTMENT
←OPEN→

4½"

¾"

½" GLIDE CLEAR-ANCE

TAPE STORAGE DRAWER

5½"

½" GAP

6"

⅛"

25⅞"

TOUCH LATCH

⅛" CLEARANCE

VIDEO CAMERA
ETC.
STORAGE COMPARTMENT

11½"

HINGES

2⅜"

INSIDE DIMENSION
19"

FRONT VIEW

14¾"

OPEN VCR

½" FINGER HOLD

DRAWER

SEE DETAIL

TOUCH LATCH

14"

¼ PLY BACK

18⅜"

2⅛" DIA HOLE IN BACK

26" OVER -ALL

BOTTOM SHELF

HINGE

DETAIL

SIDE SECTION VIEW

Fig. 10

45° BEVEL

Fig. 9

5½"

½"×17" DIVIDER

¼" PLY. BOTTOM

1¾"

3½"

¼"

DRAWER DETAIL
SIDE SECTION

HINGE DETAIL

glue inside the parallel pencil lines and slipping the shelves into the marked positions. Nail the sides and the back to the two shelves (see Fig. 5).

Stand the unit up and fit the rabbeted top piece onto the sides (see Fig. 6). If possible, don't use nails on the top piece, where they will show. Instead, use glue and bar clamps, waiting several hours for the glue to dry.

While the glue is drying, cut the ½x4 clear pine board into two 17-inch pieces for the front and back and two 14-inch pieces for the sides of the drawer. With a table saw, cut a ¼x¼-inch dado, ¼ inch up from the bottom edge of each piece. Fit the 13½x17½-inch ¼-inch plywood drawer bottom into the ¼-inch dado and glue and nail the pieces together to form a box (see Fig. 7).

From the remaining ½x4 pine board, rip a 1¾-inch-wide by 17-inch-long piece for the drawer divider. Glue and nail the divider in place, using 1¼-inch annular panel nails, and positioning it 7¾ inches in from the front of the drawer (see Fig. 8, Drawer Top View).

The drawer slides we recommend are economical bottom-mounted slides most often used on kitchen drawers. **NOTE:** The drawer slides are mounted to the bottom edge of the drawer box. Position the bottom of the other half of the slide on the inside cabinet wall, 6 inches down from the underneath side of the top shelf. Since the drawer face is only 5½ inches tall, this will create a ½-inch space above the drawer for a finger hold to open the drawer (see Figs. 8 & 9). Mount the slides according to the instructions, and slide the drawer into the case. After making sure that the drawer fits well and slides smoothly, glue and clamp the beveled true front onto the false front, making sure that the front of the drawer is aligned perfectly with the sides of the unit.

Attach the door to the bottom shelf by screwing a pair of 1½x2-inch butt hinges to the door and to the bottom shelf (see Fig. 10). To hold the door in place, install a touch latch to the side wall of the case (see Fig. 8, Front View & Storage Stool, page 100, Fig. 10, Touch Latch Detail).

Use a 2⅛-inch-diameter hole saw to cut a hole in the back piece, so the electrical cords can fit through the back and into the power bar.

Fill any nail holes with wood putty, then sand the unit with 120- and 220-grit sandpaper. Finish it with a clear waterborne acrylic urethane.

Outdoor, Garden & Sports Equipment Storage

Deck- & Pool-Cushion Storage Bench

T HIS STURDY, WATERPROOF storage bench can be filled with several deck and pool cushions and is large enough to store a chaise lounge pillow. It could also be used for outdoor sports equipment, such as croquet mallets, tennis and badminton rackets or baseball mitts. Set on casters, the unit can be moved around and even used as a bench on your deck or patio. The top of ours is covered with a bright blue waterproof canvas stuffed with an inch of washable Fiberfill, which makes

MATERIALS LIST

Quantity	Size	Description	Location or Use
1 sheet	4x8 feet	½-inch A-C exterior plywood	top, bottom, cleat
32	14 inches	1x6 clear T&G cedar	front, back, sides
4	24 inches	1x2 #2 pine	box supports
4	52 inches	1x2 #2 pine	box supports
2	25¾ inches	1x2 #2 pine	top edging
2	56¾ inches	1x2 #2 pine	top edging
2	56¾ inches	⅛x¾-inch cedar	top cedar strips
2	25¾ inches	⅛x¾-inch cedar	top cedar strips
1 bottle	8 ounces	waterproof glue	
6	¾-inch	#6 galvanized deck screws	cleat
1 box	1¼-inch	#8 galvanized deck screws	
1 box	2-inch	galvanized finish nails	
1 box	1½-inch	galvanized finish nails	
1 box	¾-inch	galvanized wire nails	
1 box	⅜-inch	staples	
1 sheet each	60-, 120- & 220-grit	sandpaper	
1 pkg.		Fiberfill	top cover filling
1	3x5 feet	waterproof awning canvas	top cover
4	1½-inch-dia.	plate-type casters	
1 quart		clear waterproof sealer	

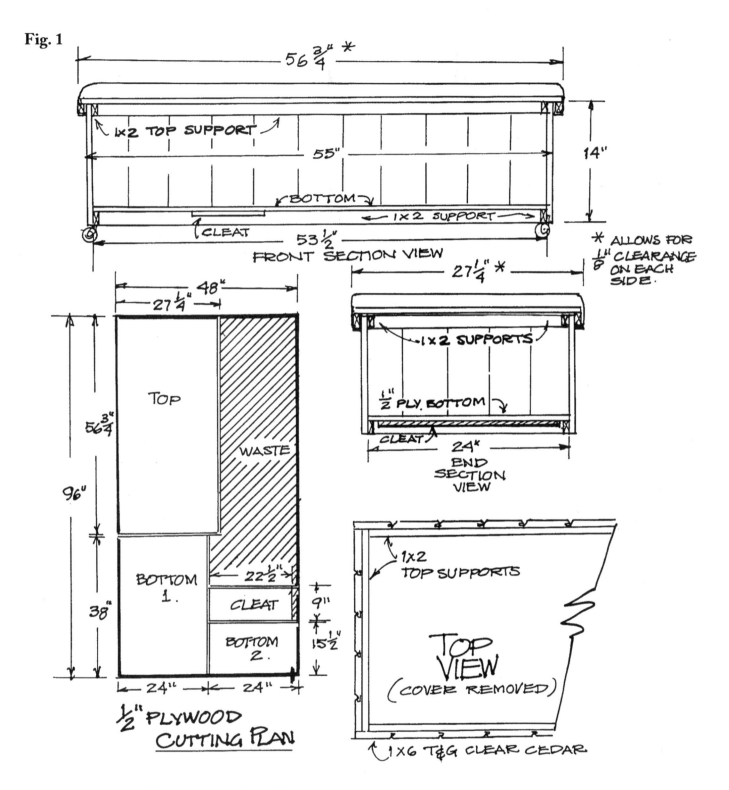

Fig. 1

56 ¾" *

1x2 TOP SUPPORT

55"

14"

BOTTOM

CLEAT   53 ½"   ← 1x2 SUPPORT →

FRONT SECTION VIEW

* ALLOWS FOR ⅛" CLEARANCE ON EACH SIDE.

27 ¼" *

1x2 SUPPORTS

½" PLY. BOTTOM

CLEAT   24"

END SECTION VIEW

48"

27 ¼"

TOP

56 ¾"

96"

WASTE

22 ½"

BOTTOM 1.

CLEAT   9"

38"

BOTTOM 2.   15 ¼"

24"   24"

½" PLYWOOD CUTTING PLAN

1x2 TOP SUPPORTS

TOP VIEW (COVER REMOVED)

1x6 T&G CLEAR CEDAR.

the bench soft enough to sit on comfortably, yet keeps it easy to maintain.

Begin by cutting out the pieces from a full sheet of ½-inch A-C exterior plywood, following the dimensions shown on the Cutting Plan (see Fig. 1). Since there is not enough room to cut the bottom panel in one piece, it is necessary to cut it in two pieces and join them together with a 9x22½-inch plywood cleat. Place the cleat over the two bottom pieces, allowing a ¾-inch space on each end of the cleat for the 1x2 supports to fit into later. Glue and screw the cleat to the bottom pieces, using waterproof glue and ¾-inch galvanized deck screws (see Fig. 2).

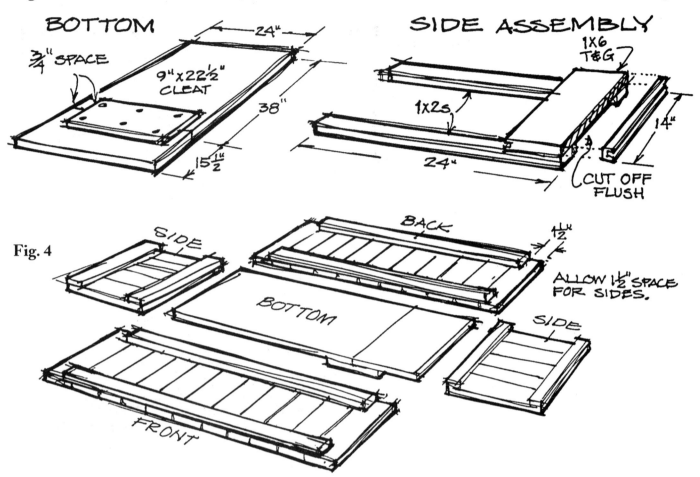

Fig. 4

Cut four 24-inch-long pieces of 1x2 to make the side supports and four 52-inch-long pieces of 1x2 to make the front and back supports. Build the two sides of the box first. Lay two pieces of 1x2 14 inches apart from outside edge to outside edge, parallel to the front edge of your worktable. Cut one 14-inch-long piece of 1x6 clear T&G cedar and cut off the "tongue" so that the side is square. Place the board over the two 1x2s so that the ends of the 1x6 are flush with the 1x2 sides and ends. Check the corners for square, and glue the 1x6 down to the 1x2s (see Fig. 3). Keep adding 1x6s, gluing them as you proceed, and lightly tapping the tongue of each piece into the groove of the previous one, using a scrap block of wood, until you reach the other end. Rip the last board, if necessary, so that the 1x6 T&G board is square and flush with the ends of the 1x2s. Build the other side of the box in the same manner.

The front and back of the box are constructed in the same way, except you allow a 1½-inch overlap at each end of the 52-inch-long 1x2 supports (see Fig. 4).

Once the glue has dried, stand the pieces up to see if they fit together perfectly, with the front and back pieces overlapping the side pieces. For added strength, lay the four side pieces down so the 1x2s face up and screw one 1¼-inch galvanized deck screw through the 1x2 and into the back of each 1x6 T&G.

To assemble the pieces, apply a bead of glue to the four corners and the top edge of the bottom 1x2 supports. With the help of an assistant, set the pieces up into position, including the bottom. Use bar clamps to hold the pieces together while the glue is drying. If bar clamps are not available, wrap rope around the box, slipping wedges between the rope and the sides to tighten up the rope and distribute the pressure (see Fig. 5).

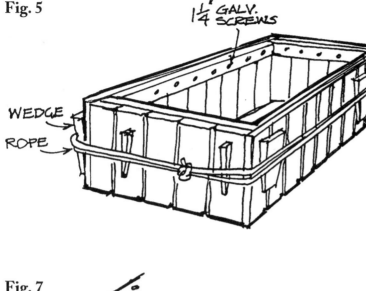

Fig. 5

1¼" GALV. SCREWS

WEDGE

ROPE

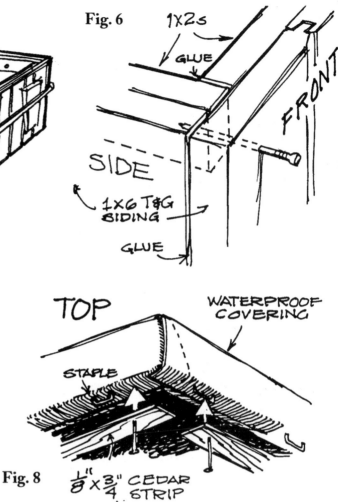

Fig. 6

1x2s

GLUE

SIDE

FRONT

1x6 T&G SIDING

GLUE

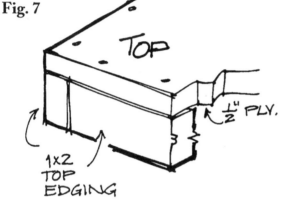

Fig. 7

TOP

½" PLY.

1x2 TOP EDGING

Fig. 8

TOP

WATERPROOF COVERING

STAPLE

⅛"x¾" CEDAR STRIP

Hammer one 2-inch galvanized finish nail through each top and bottom corner and into the ends of the 1x2s (see Fig. 6).

Sand the outside surfaces, using 60-, 120- and 220-grit sandpaper and an electric palm sander. **NOTE:** While working on the box, place a piece of carpet underneath to prevent scratching and denting the soft surface of the cedar. Finish it with a clear waterproof sealer, such as Thompson's Waterseal.

Lay the top piece of ½-inch plywood over the box, making sure that it overlaps the sides at each end by more than ¾ inch (to allow for the thickness of the top 1x2 edge and ⅛ inch clearance). Cut two pieces of 1x2 top edging, each measuring 25¾ inches, and two more measuring 56¾ inches. Using two 1½-inch galvanized finish nails at each corner, fasten the 1x2 edge pieces together to form a rectan-

gle, with the two larger pieces overlapping the ends of the two shorter pieces. Then glue and nail the plywood top to these edge pieces (see Fig. 7), again using 1½-inch galvanized finish nails.

Cover the top with 1-inch Fiberfill and then a waterproof canvas-type material, such as Sunbrella. Staple the covering to the 1x2 edge pieces on the underneath side of the top. Then cover the staples with ⅛x¾-inch strips of cedar, nailed through the covering and into the bottom edge of the 1x2 edge pieces (see Fig. 8), using ¾-inch galvanized wire nails.

Attach four 1½-inch-diameter plate-type casters by screwing them into the bottom corners of the storage box, making sure that each caster plate is flush with the outside corner of the box.

Hose House

BEFORE WE BUILT THIS HOSE HOUSE, our garden hose was an eyesore, always lying on the ground twisted up in a haphazard fashion, often underfoot, and difficult to untangle. We tried coiling it and hanging it on pegs that were drilled into the side of the house, but this proved to be an unsatisfactory solution, as did the metal hangers sold in garden stores, which are unattractive and cumbersome. This simple wooden box was the answer. The hose house attaches to the outside wall of our house, and once all the wood weathered to a natural gray, it was barely noticeable, blending in with the exterior shingles of the house. Connected to an outdoor spigot through a hole in the bottom of the box, the hose coils easily into the box and can be quickly reeled out without kinking. The interior shelf compartment at the top of the hose house can be used to hold spare nozzles, a sprinkler head and other similar items.

Using the Cutting Plan as your guide (see Fig. 1), begin by cutting out the sides, top shelf and bottom pieces from an 8-foot-long piece of 1x8 cedar.

Fig. 1

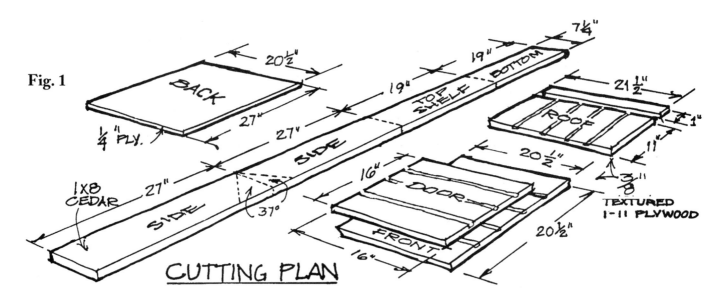

CUTTING PLAN

MATERIALS LIST

Quantity	Size	Description	Location or Use
1	8 feet	1x8 #2 cedar	sides, top & bottom
1	20½x20½ inches	⅜-inch textured (T1-11) plywood with 4-inch grooves o.c.	front
1	16x16 inches	⅜-inch T1-11 plywood	door
1	12x21½ inches	⅜-inch T1-11 plywood	roof
1	20½x27 inches	¼-inch plywood	back
1	19½ inches	1x2 #2 pine	top ledge
20	18 inches	red cedar shingles (optional)	roof
1 pair	2x2-inch	butt hinges	roof
1 pair	⅜-inch	offset hinges	door
1	1¼-inch	knob	door
1		nylon roller friction catch	door
1 tube		PL-200 construction adhesive	
1 box	2-inch	galvanized finish nails	
1 box	1-inch	galvanized wire nails	
1 sheet	60-grit	sandpaper	
1	7x21 inches	aluminum flashing (optional)	roof

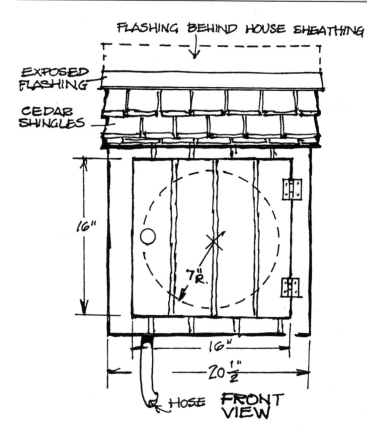

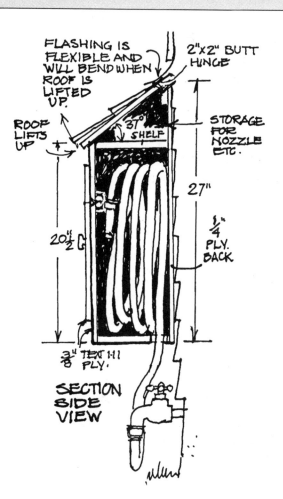

Cut the front, door and roof pieces out of ⅜-inch textured (T1-11) plywood.

Assemble the box by gluing, clamping and nailing the side pieces to the bottom and the top shelf pieces, using the PL-200 construction adhesive and 2-inch galvanized finish nails placed every 2 inches. **TIP:** To keep the wood from moving while you are nailing into it, clamp a solid block of wood, such as a 2x4, to your worktable to act as a brace (see Fig. 2).

Fig. 2

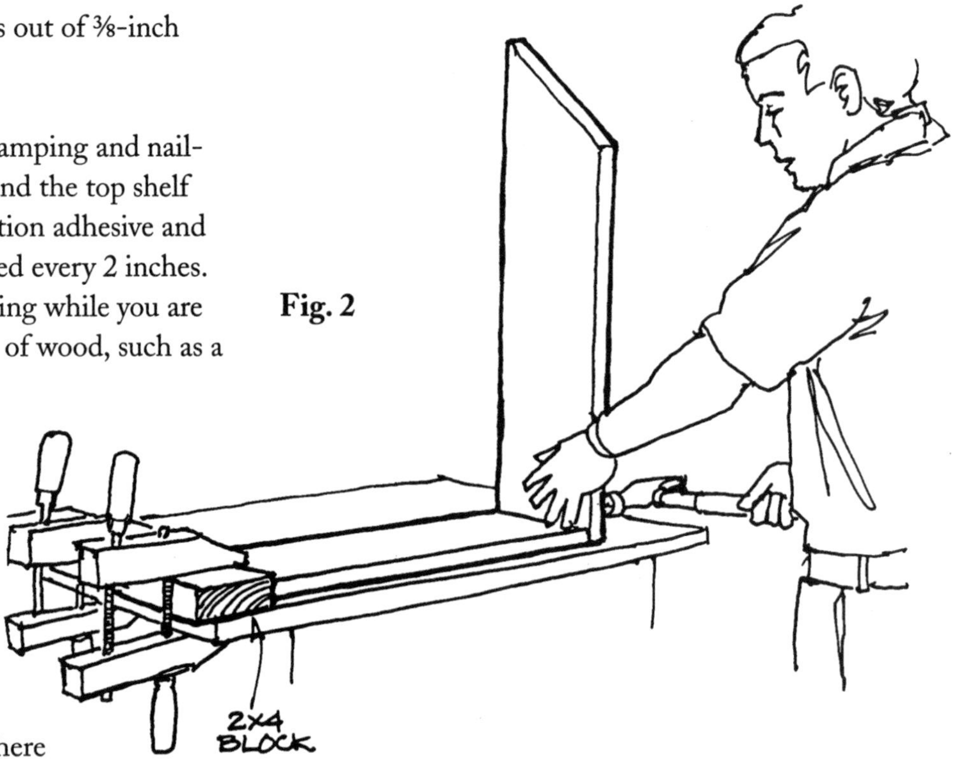

2x4 BLOCK

Cut a 14-inch-diameter circle out of the 20½x20½-inch front piece using an electric jigsaw. First, find the center of the front piece by drawing two lines, connecting the opposite corners of the board. The point where the lines intersect marks the center (see Fig. 3). To scribe the circle, make a beam compass out of a piece of scrap wood. Drill a ³⁄₃₂-inch pilot hole in one end of the scrap wood. Measure over 7 inches from this hole and drill a second hole ⁵⁄₁₆ inch in diameter. Place a finish nail in the first hole and a pencil in the second hole, then place the nail in the center of the front piece. Use the compass to draw the 14-inch-diameter circle (see Fig. 3).

Fig. 3

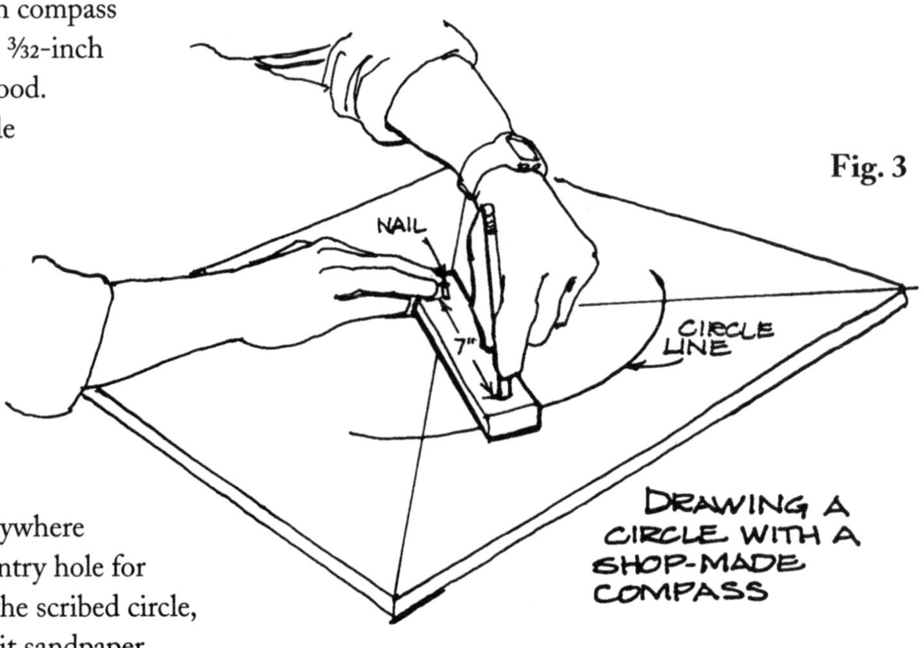

NAIL

7"

CIRCLE LINE

DRAWING A CIRCLE WITH A SHOP-MADE COMPASS

Drill a ⅜-inch-diameter hole anywhere inside the circle and use this as an entry hole for the jigsaw blade. After cutting out the scribed circle, sand the edges smooth, using 60-grit sandpaper.

Bevel the top edge of the front piece by running it through a table saw with the blade set at 37 degrees. Glue and nail the front panel to the box using 2-inch galvanized finish nails.

Glue and nail the 20½x27-inch ¼-inch plywood back to the box, using 1-inch galvanized wire nails.

To reinforce the back, cut a 19½-inch-long piece of 1x2, and bevel the top edge at a 37-degree angle. Glue, clamp and nail it to the top of the back piece, using 1-inch galvanized wire nails (see Fig. 4).

To make the roof, cut a 1-inch strip off the rear of the roof piece and glue and nail it to the beveled edge of the 1x2. Install a pair of 2x2-inch butt

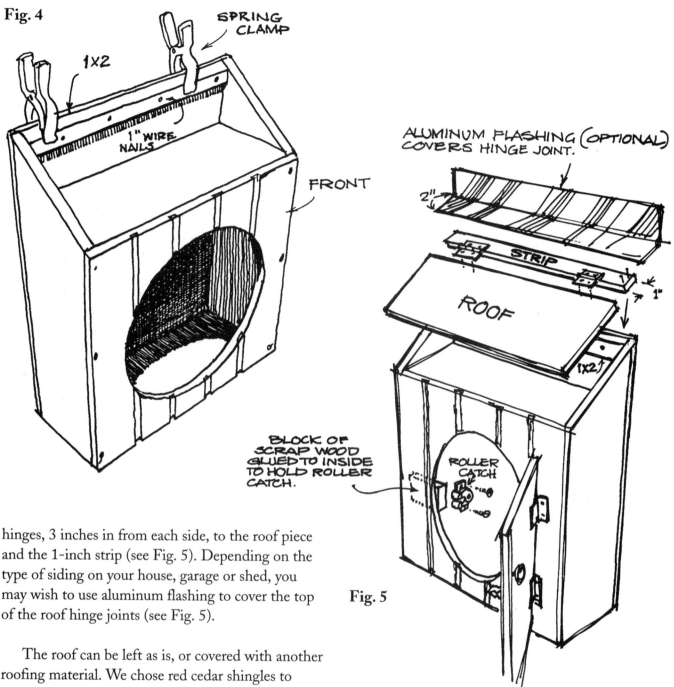

Fig. 4

SPRING CLAMP

1X2

1" WIRE NAILS

FRONT

BLOCK OF SCRAP WOOD GLUED TO INSIDE TO HOLD ROLLER CATCH.

ALUMINUM FLASHING (OPTIONAL) COVERS HINGE JOINT.

2"

STRIP

ROOF

1"

1X2

ROLLER CATCH

Fig. 5

hinges, 3 inches in from each side, to the roof piece and the 1-inch strip (see Fig. 5). Depending on the type of siding on your house, garage or shed, you may wish to use aluminum flashing to cover the top of the roof hinge joints (see Fig. 5).

The roof can be left as is, or covered with another roofing material. We chose red cedar shingles to match our house. If you decide to do this as well, cut 20 shingles, each 3½ inches wide and 10½ inches long, to make two rows, with the first row doubled. Glue and nail them to the plywood roof, staggering the joints, using PL-200 construction adhesive and 1-inch galvanized wire nails.

Install the pair of ⅜-inch offset hinges to the

door and mount it to the box so that it covers the circular hole. Add the knob and roller catch as shown in Fig. 5.

To provide access for the hose, drill a 1½-inch-diameter hole in the bottom of the hose house.

Trash Shed

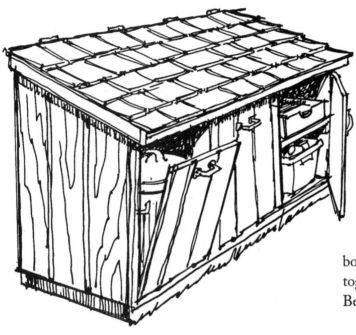

T HIS SORELY NEEDED TRASH SHED replaced our former one, which was jerry-rigged from salvaged wood and became a favorite meeting spot for raccoons and mice. With new recycling laws and wildlife encroaching ever closer to suburban areas, a trash shed must be carefully thought out. We designed a three-sectioned one that accommodates two 21-inch-diameter plastic garbage pails (one for wet garbage and one for dry), and a recycling cabinet that contains a shelf for newspaper storage and a bin underneath for bottles and cans. **NOTE:** This project is mainly put together using screws rather than nails as fasteners. Besides being stronger, screws are easier to install

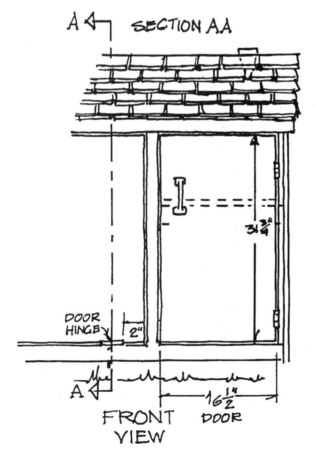

SECTION AA

DOOR HINGE

2"

3¾"

16½" DOOR

FRONT VIEW

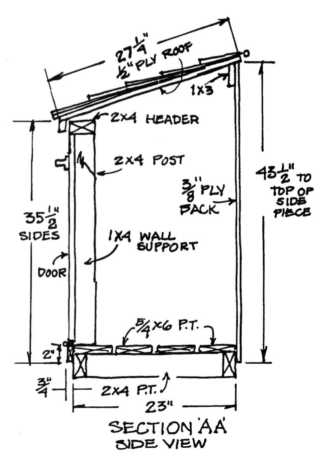

SECTION AA

27¼" ½" PLY ROOF

1×3

2×4 HEADER

2×4 POST

⅜" PLY BACK

43½" TO TOP OF SIDE PIECE

35¼" SIDES

1×4 WALL SUPPORT

DOOR

5/4×6 P.T.

2"

¾"

2×4 P.T.

23"

SECTION 'AA' SIDE VIEW

MATERIALS LIST

Quantity	Size	Description	Location or Use
3	6 feet	2x4 pressure-treated (P.T.) lumber	base frame
4	6 feet	5/4x6 pressure-treated (P.T.) decking	base
1	12 feet	2x4 #2 construction fir	posts, headers
1 sheet	4x8 feet	5/8-inch textured (T1-11) plywood with 8-inch grooves	doors, sides
2 sheets	4x8 feet	1/2-inch A-C plywood	roof, bins, cleats, shelf
1 sheet	4x8 feet	3/8-inch A-C plywood	back
1	15½x21½ inches	1/4-inch plywood	box bottom (optional)
1	6 feet	1x3 #2 pine	back support
2	8 feet	1x4 #2 pine	side supports, shelf cleats
1	8 feet	1x6 #2 cedar	door ledge & roof trim
1	6 feet	1x8 #2 pine	box sides (optional)
1 bundle	18 inches	red cedar shingles	roof
1 bottle	8 ounces	waterproof glue	
1 box	2½-inch	#10 galvanized deck screws	
1 box	1½-inch	#8 galvanized deck screws	
1 box	1-inch	#6 galvanized deck screws	
1 box	1-inch	galvanized wire nails	bin
1 box	1⅛-inch	galvanized common nails	roof
2 pairs	5½-inch	galvanized strap hinges	roof (optional)
3 pairs	2x2-inch	galvanized butt hinges	doors
3	5½-inch	galvanized handles	doors
1		nylon roller friction catch	door
1	2x6 feet	screening	base (optional)
1 quart		clear waterproof sealer (optional)	

(using an electric drill with a Phillips bit) and are also easier to remove if you make a mistake.

Begin by building the frame for the base out of the 2x4 pressure-treated (P.T.) lumber. Cut three 20-inch-long pieces and two 69-inch-long pieces. Screw the 69-inch front and back pieces to the two 20-inch side pieces, using 2½-inch galvanized deck screws (see Fig. 1). Screw the third 20-inch-long piece in the center to provide support for the decking.

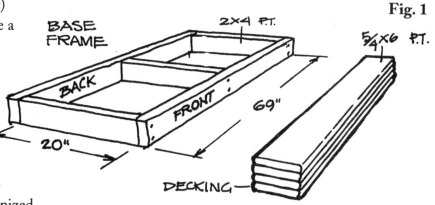

Fig. 1

Cut four pieces of 5/4x6 P.T. decking, each 69 inches long, for the base decking. Use 1½-inch galvanized deck screws to screw the decking to the base,

Fig. 2

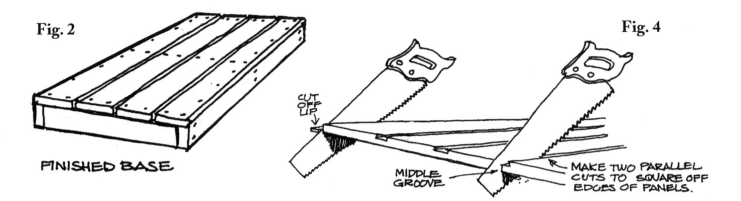

FINISHED BASE

Fig. 4

CUT OFF LIP

MIDDLE GROOVE

MAKE TWO PARALLEL CUTS TO SQUARE OFF EDGES OF PANELS.

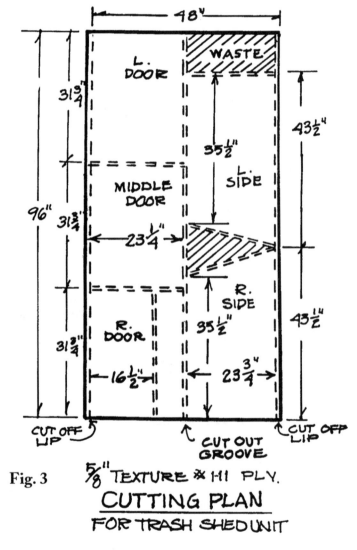

Fig. 3

48"

L. DOOR

WASTE

31¾"

35½"

MIDDLE DOOR

L. SIDE

96"   31¾"

23¼"

43½"

R. SIDE

R. DOOR

35½"

31¾"

16½"

23¾"

43½"

CUT OFF LIP

CUT OUT GROOVE

CUT OFF LIP

⅝" TEXTURE X H1 PLY.
CUTTING PLAN
FOR TRASH SHED UNIT

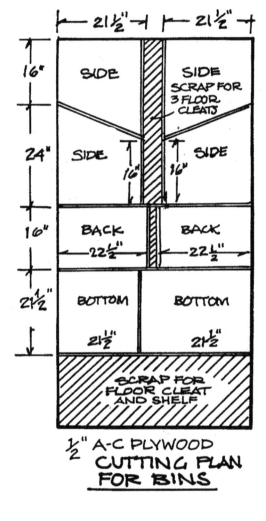

21½"   21½"

16"   SIDE   SIDE
              SCRAP FOR
              3 FLOOR
              CLEATS

24"   SIDE   SIDE
      16"   16"

16"   BACK   BACK
      22½"   22½"

2½"   BOTTOM   BOTTOM
      21½"   21½"

SCRAP FOR FLOOR CLEAT AND SHELF

½" A-C PLYWOOD
CUTTING PLAN
FOR BINS

beginning with the two outer boards and followed by the two middle boards spaced evenly between them. Place two screws at the end and middle of each board and six more screws running lengthwise on each of the two outer boards (see Fig. 2). **TIP:** Tack screening to the underside of the decking as an extra deterrent against rodents and insects.

Referring to the Cutting Plans for the plywood (see Fig. 3), cut the three doors and two side pieces out of the sheet of ⅝-inch textured (T1-11) plywood, using a hand or portable circular saw with a blade for cutting plywood. This type of plywood has a ½-inch lip on each side edge, which needs to be sawed off (see Fig. 4). Also make two cuts in the

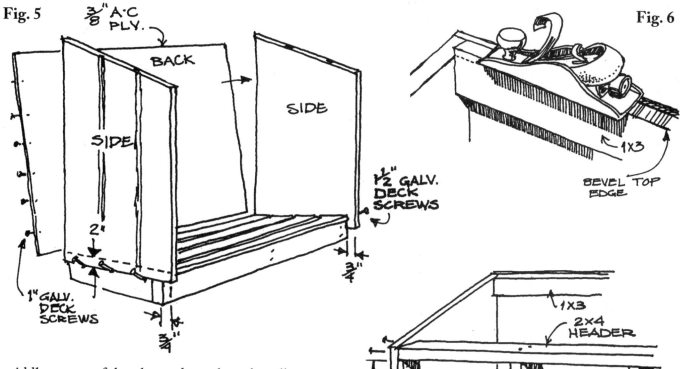

Fig. 5

⅜" A-C PLY.

BACK

SIDE

SIDE

½" GALV. DECK SCREWS

2"

¾"

1" GALV. DECK SCREWS

¾"

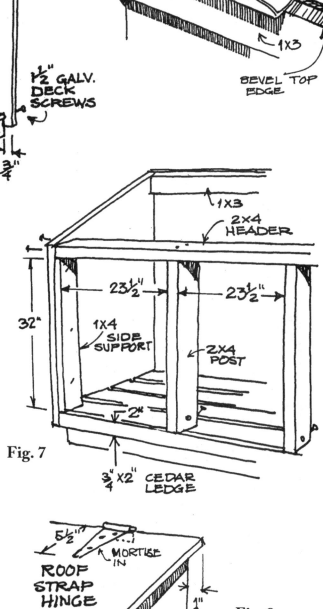

Fig. 6

1x3

BEVEL TOP EDGE

1x3

2x4 HEADER

23½"   23½"

32"

1x4 SIDE SUPPORT

2x4 POST

2"

Fig. 7

¾"x2" CEDAR LEDGE

5½"

MORTISE IN

ROOF STRAP HINGE

1"

Fig. 8

middle groove of the plywood panel, so that all the edges are square. This will leave you with two 8-foot-long pieces of plywood: one 23¼ inches wide, from which you cut the three doors, and one 23¾ inches wide, from which you cut the two sides of the trash shed.

To make the side assembly easier, hammer three nails into the base, and use them as a ledge on which to rest the side panel while you are drilling in the screws (see Fig. 5). Drill three screws through the side panel into the base. Use 1½-inch galvanized deck screws, and allow the sides to overlap the front of the base by ¾ inch.

Cut the 43½x70¼-inch back piece from the sheet of ⅜-inch A-C plywood. Screw it to the back edges of the side pieces and to the base, using 1-inch galvanized deck screws placed 6 inches apart (see Fig. 5). To strengthen the back piece, cut a 69-inch-long 1x3 and screw it to the inside top of the back piece, using 1-inch galvanized deck screws. Using a block plane, bevel the top edge of the 1x3 and the ⅜-inch plywood back piece to match the angle of the two sides (see Fig. 6). To strengthen the sides, cut two pieces of 1x4 #2 pine, each 32 inches long, and screw them to the front inside edges of the sides,

placing 1-inch galvanized deck screws 6 inches apart (see Fig. 7). Join the sides together with a 2x4 #2 fir header, cut 69 inches long. Place the 2x4 on top of the 1x4 side supports and drill two 2½-inch galvanized deck screws through each side and into the end of the header (see Fig. 7). **NOTE:** Before screwing the screws all the way in, make sure the

Fig. 9

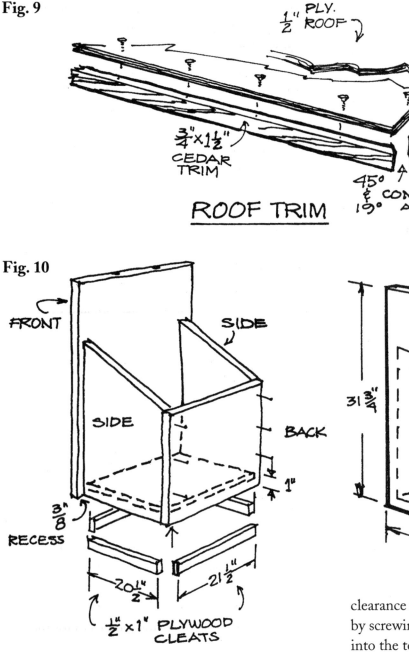

½" PLY.
ROOF

19°

¾"×1½"
CEDAR
TRIM

45°
&
19° COMPOUND
ANGLE
CUT

ROOF TRIM

Fig. 10

FRONT

SIDE

SIDE

BACK

1"

3/8
RECESS

20½"

21½"

½"×1" PLYWOOD
CLEATS

Fig. 10A

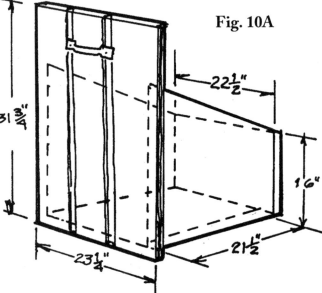

31¾"

22½"

16"

23¼"

21½"

plywood doors will fit under the 2x4 header, with a ⅛-inch clearance.

Construct a ledge by ripping a 2-inch-wide piece off the 8-foot cedar 1x6 and cutting it 69 inches long. Screw it to the front edge of the base and the P.T. decking (see Fig. 7). This will be the support on which the doors will be hinged. Cut two 32-inch-long support posts out of the remaining piece of 2x4 #2 fir. Install one of the 2x4 posts so it is 23½ inches from the 1x4 side support. This allows for ⅛-inch

clearance on either side of the door. Attach the post by screwing two 2½-inch galvanized deck screws into the top and two screws at an angle through the post and into the base (see Fig. 7). Do the same for the second post, placing it 23½ inches from the first one. Temporarily hold the left and middle doors in place to determine the exact dimension of the right door. Mark and cut this third door, which should be approximately 16½ inches wide.

From one 4x8 sheet of ½-inch A-C plywood, cut the 27¼x72⅜-inch roof panel. Position the roof panel on top of the shed, allowing for a 1-inch overlap at each end, and attach it using two pairs of 5½-inch strap hinges, equidistantly spaced.

Mortise out the roof panel so that the hinges lie flush with the top of the plywood (see Fig. 8). **NOTE:** Although many trash sheds are hinged at the top (as shown here), you may want to eliminate the hinges and simply nail the roof panel down permanently.

Trim the front of the roof by ripping the 8-foot 1x6 cedar into two more strips, each 1½ inches wide. Miter each end of one of these pieces at a 45-degree angle and screw it to the underside of the front edge of the roof, placing the 1½-inch galvanized deck screws 8 inches apart (see Fig. 9). To trim the sides of the roof, cut the other ¾x1½-inch strip into two pieces, each 27¼ inches long. Miter the back ends of each side piece at a 19-degree angle and the front ends at a 45-degree and 19-degree compound angle cut to meet the front trim. Screw the side trim in place by drilling the 1½-inch galvanized deck screws through the roof and into the top edge of the trim pieces.

To attach the right front door to the shed, mortise one pair of 2x2 butt hinges to the door and door frame. **TIP:** Using an awl or nail to start the screw holes makes it easier to drill in the screws. Attach a nylon roller friction catch to the 2x4 post and screw a 5½-inch galvanized handle to the front of the door.

The remaining two doors can be attached to the shed in the same fashion; however, using tilt-out bins instead of doors (as we have done) eliminates having to remove and replace the garbage cans every time you put trash into them.

To build the two tilt-out bins, cut out the pieces to the dimensions shown in the Cutting Plan for the ½-inch A-C plywood (see Fig. 3). Construct the bins by gluing and nailing the back pieces to the sides and the bottom. Note that the sides are recessed ⅜ inch in from the side edges of the front panel/door, to allow for clearance (see Fig. 10).

From the leftover ½-inch plywood, cut out eight cleats to support the floor of the two bins:

four pieces measuring 1x21½ inches and four pieces measuring 1x20½ inches. Glue and then nail four cleats around the bottom inside perimeter of each bin, hammering 1-inch galvanized wire nails from the inside of the bin. To do this, place a bead of waterproof glue on the top edge of the cleats, lay the floor pieces against the glue and hammer the nails through the floor inside the bin and into the cleats, spacing the nails every 3 inches.

To hinge the two bins to the shed unit so they can easily pivot open, use a pair of 2x2-inch galvanized butt hinges on each bin door, placed 2 inches in from each side. Use a piece of scrap wood or a rock to prop open the door while you attach half of each hinge to the bottom of each bin and the other half of each hinge to the 2-inch cedar ledge (see Fig. 11).

For the compartment behind the right door, build two shelf supports by cutting and screwing two 22-inch cleats, cut from the remaining 1x4 pine, to the sides of the compartment, 9 inches from the top. To make the shelf, cut a 15½x22-inch piece of ½-inch plywood and lay it on top of the cleats (see Fig. 12).

Buy a plastic bin that fits in the bottom of the compartment to hold plastic and glass bottles. Either use a cardboard box or, if you want to go all out, build a wooden box to hold newspapers in the top compartment. Use the 6-foot-long 1x8 for the

Fig. 11

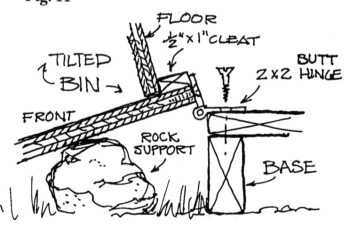

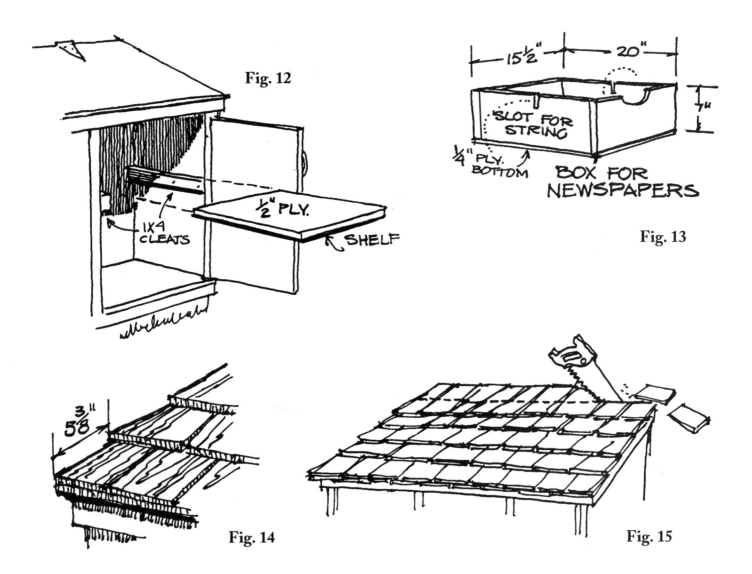

Fig. 12

Fig. 13

Fig. 14

Fig. 15

15½-inch front and back and 20-inch sides, and a 15½x21½-inch piece of ¼-inch plywood for the bottom. Cut a shallow 2-inch-deep hand hold in the top front of the box, using the curve of a gallon can of paint as your guide. To facilitate tying up the newspapers, we cut a 1½-inch slot in the middle of each side of the box, to hold string (see Fig. 13).

Shingle the top of the garbage shed, using 18-inch red cedar shingles, allowing a 5⅜-inch exposure from one row of shingles to the next (see Fig. 14). Double the first row, and stagger the joints so that the shingles never line up from row to row. Use 1⅛-inch galvanized common nails, two to each shingle. Allow the shingles to overlap at the top and cut them off when you have finished shingling the entire roof (see Fig. 15).

If desired, finish the shed with a clear waterproof sealer.

Bulk Storage Bins

THESE PRACTICAL storage bins eliminate the unsightly, heavy bags of rock salt, charcoal, peat moss, birdseed, pet food and other products that often get piled on top of each other in the garage or shed. The bins keep these bulk supplies up off the ground, protecting them from moisture and making it more difficult for mice and other small animals to have access to the contents. By swinging open the hinged door at the bottom of each bin, you can easily control how much comes out. There's just enough space below the bins to put a bucket or other container, and the slanted false bottom in each bin allows the contents to pour out easily.

Using the measurements shown on the Cutting Plan as your guide (see Fig. 1), cut out all the pieces from the ¾-inch exterior plywood.

		MATERIALS LIST	
Quantity	**Size**	**Description**	**Location or Use**
1 sheet	4x8 feet	¾-inch exterior plywood	top, false bottom, sides, back, front, hinge strip, partitions, doors
1	8 feet	1x2 #2 pine	trim
3	1½x3-inch	galvanized butt hinges	top
4	¾x3-inch	galvanized butt hinges	doors
4	2-inch	galvanized hooks & eyes	
4	1⅛-inch-diameter	wood pulls	
1 box	1½-inch	#8 galvanized deck screws	bins
1 box	1½-inch	galvanized finish nails	trim
1 bottle	8 ounces	waterproof glue	
3	3-inch	½-inch-diameter lag bolts	
1	8x12 inches	aluminum flashing	
1 quart		paint or waterproof stain	

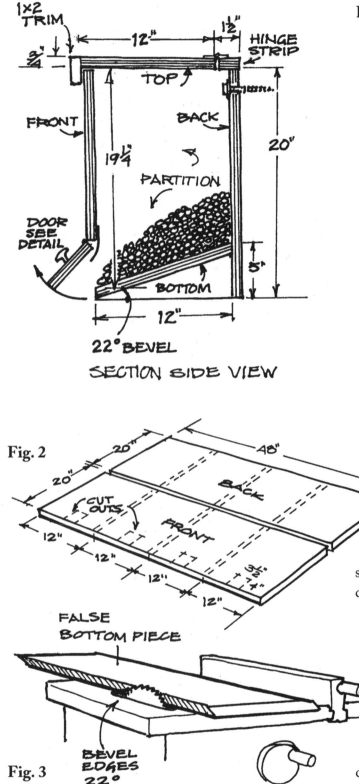

1×2 TRIM

12" 1½" HINGE STRIP

¾"

TOP

FRONT   BACK

19¼"   20"

PARTITION

DOOR SEE DETAIL

BOTTOM   5"

12"

22° BEVEL

SECTION SIDE VIEW

Fig. 2

20"   48"

20"

12"   BACK

12"   FRONT

12"

12"

CUT OUTS

3½" 7"

FALSE BOTTOM PIECE

BEVEL EDGES 22°

Fig. 3

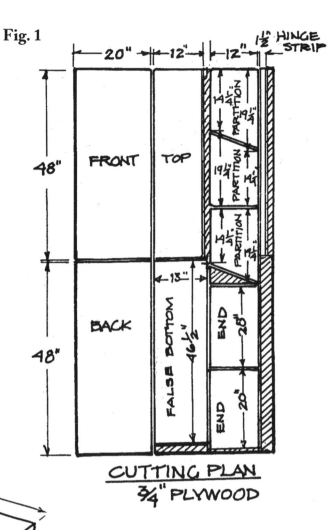

Fig. 1

20"   12"   12"   1½" HINGE STRIP

48"   FRONT   TOP

19¼" PARTITION   14¼"

19¼" PARTITION   14¼"

48"   BACK   FALSE BOTTOM 46½"   END 28"   END 20"

13"

CUTTING PLAN
¾" PLYWOOD

Lay the front and the back pieces face down and mark where the partitions will go. Make two parallel lines, ¾ inch apart, every 12 inches (see Fig. 2). On the bottom of the front piece, mark and make a

3½x4-inch cutout in the center of each bin location, using an electric jigsaw fitted with a scroll blade. Save the pieces—these will become the doors of the bins.

Set the table saw blade at a 22-degree angle and rip the two outside long edges of the false bottom piece so that they are beveled at a 22-degree angle (see Fig. 3).

To assemble the bins, screw the front and the back to the two ends, using 1½-inch galvanized deck screws, spaced every 3 inches (see Fig. 4). Turn the assembly right side up and glue and screw the beveled false bottom piece to the inside of the front and back, so that it rests at a 22-degree angle (see Fig. 5 & this page, Section Side View). Using the ¾-inch parallel marks as your guide, glue and screw the three partitions in place (see Fig. 5).

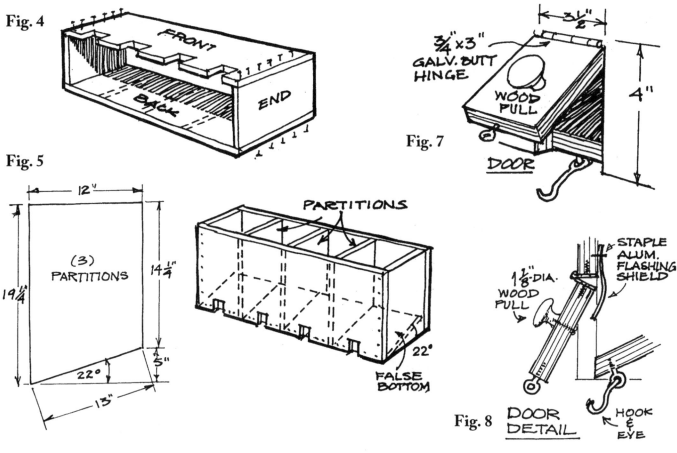

Fig. 4

FRONT

END

BACK

Fig. 7

3/4"x3"
GALV. BUTT
HINGE

3½"

WOOD
PULL

4"

DOOR

Fig. 5

12"

(3)
PARTITIONS

14¼"

19¼"

22°

5"

13"

PARTITIONS

PARTITIONS

22°

FALSE
BOTTOM

STAPLE
ALUM.
FLASHING
SHIELD

1⅛" DIA.
WOOD
PULL

Fig. 8   DOOR
DETAIL

HOOK
&
EYE

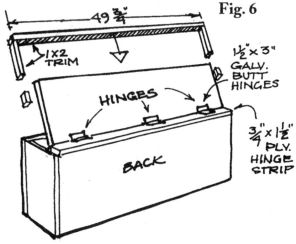

Fig. 6

49¾"

1x2
TRIM

1½"x3"
GALV.
BUTT
HINGES

HINGES

BACK

¾"x1½"
PLY.
HINGE
STRIP

To trim the top, cut the 8-foot 1x2 #2 pine into five pieces: one 49¾ inches, two 12 inches, and two 1½ inches. Glue and nail the trim to the top edges, using 1½-inch galvanized finish nails (see Fig. 6).

Screw the 1½-inch-wide hinge strip to the back piece and attach three 1½x3-inch galvanized butt hinges to the hinge strip and the top piece (see Fig. 6). Add the 1½-inch trim pieces to the ends, using glue and 1½-inch galvanized finish nails.

Screw a ¾x3-inch galvanized butt hinge to the top of each door and to the top edge of each 3½x4-inch cutout (see Fig. 7). Bore a ⅛-inch-diameter hole in the center of each door and install a 1⅛-inch-diameter wood pull.

To prevent the contents of the bins from getting caught in the hinge, keeping the door from closing all the way, staple a sheet of thin metal flashing to the inside of each bin compartment, just above the door (see Fig. 8, Door Detail). Install a galvanized hook and eye at the bottom of each door and the bottom shelf, to keep the contents from spilling out the door.

Sand, then finish the unit with a paint or water-proof stain of your choice.

Since the storage bins can be heavy when filled, it's essential to bolt the unit to the wall, using three ½-inch-diameter lag bolts, drilled into the wall studs (see page 16, Attaching to the Wall).

Tennis Equipment Storage Rack

THIS TENNIS EQUIPMENT storage rack holds three tennis rackets and two cans of tennis balls and can be mounted on the wall of a closet, mudroom, garage, storage shed or wherever you keep your sporting equipment. If you need to store more than three rackets, just increase the length of the dowels. The tennis ball holders, made of ⅛-inch birch plywood, are designed to flex so that the tennis ball cans are held in by pressure. This is an easy, instantly rewarding project, and a simple way to neaten up a cluttered area.

Begin by cutting the back panel from the 14x28-inch piece of ½-inch plywood. Round off and sand the four corners, using 60-, 120- and 220-grit sandpaper.

Find the center of the back panel and draw a vertical line, lightly in pencil, dividing the panel lengthwise. Temporarily place your tennis racket on the center line and mark in pencil where the holding pegs should go. We found that spacing the pegs 5 inches apart, and 15 inches down from the top, fit our tennis rackets well (see Fig. 1).

To make the two slots for the ⅛-inch plywood, measure in 1½ inches from each side, make a mark and then measure 2¾ inches over from that point towards the center and make another mark. Using an electric circular saw with a ⅛-inch-wide blade, make four cuts, each 9¼ inches long, into the bottom end of the panel (see Fig. 2). **NOTE:** Test with a scrap piece of ⅛-inch plywood to make sure that the slots are the correct width.

Next, make the holes for the dowels either by using a drill press with an adjustable tilt table, or by

MATERIALS LIST

Quantity	Size	Description	Location or Use
1	14x28 inches	½-inch birch plywood	back panel
4	2½x6¼ inches	⅛-inch birch plywood	ball holder tabs
2	6½ inches	⅝-inch wood dowel	racket holder
2	2½ inches	⅝-inch wood dowel	ball holder pegs
4	2½-inch	#6 screws and wall anchors	mounting screws
1 sheet	60-grit	sandpaper	
1 sheet	120-grit	sandpaper	
1 sheet	220-grit	sandpaper	
1 bottle	8 ounces	carpenter's glue	
1 pint		clear waterborne acrylic urethane	

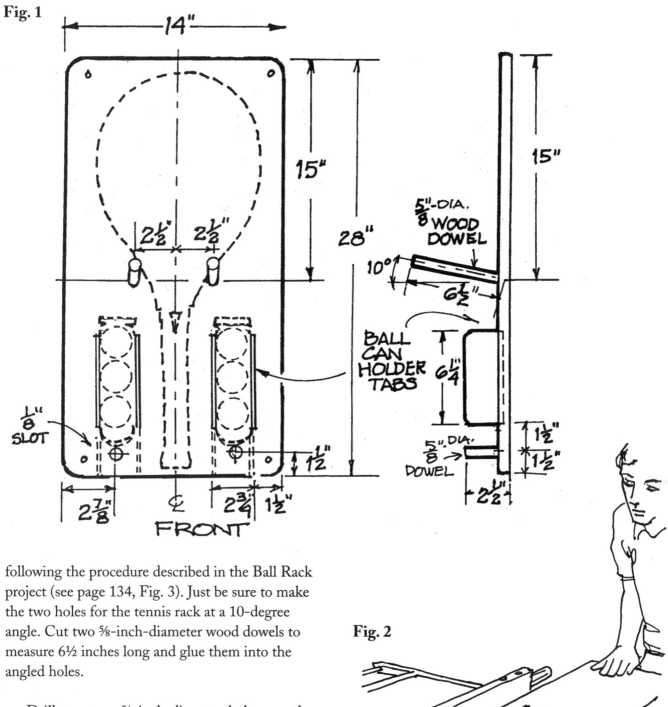

Fig. 1

14"

15"

28"

$2\frac{1}{2}$" $2\frac{1}{2}$"

$\frac{1}{8}$" SLOT

$2\frac{7}{8}$" $2\frac{3}{4}$" $1\frac{1}{2}$"

FRONT

15"

$\frac{5}{8}$"-DIA. WOOD DOWEL

10°

$6\frac{1}{2}$"

BALL CAN HOLDER TABS

$6\frac{1}{4}$"

$\frac{5}{8}$"-DIA. DOWEL

$1\frac{1}{2}$"
$1\frac{1}{2}$"

$2\frac{1}{2}$"

$1\frac{1}{2}$"

following the procedure described in the Ball Rack project (see page 134, Fig. 3). Just be sure to make the two holes for the tennis rack at a 10-degree angle. Cut two ⅝-inch-diameter wood dowels to measure 6½ inches long and glue them into the angled holes.

Drill two more ⅝-inch-diameter holes near the bottom of the panel, 2⅞ inches from each side and 1½ inches up from the bottom. These are not drilled at an angle (see Fig. 3). Cut two ⅝-inch-diameter wooden dowels to measure 2½ inches long and glue them in the holes.

Cut four 2½x6¼-inch-long tabs from the ⅛-inch plywood, round off the corners and sand with 60-, 120- and 220-grit sandpaper. Glue them in place.

Fig. 2

SLOT $9\frac{1}{4}$"

Tennis Equipment Storage Rack

Fig. 3   **Fig. 4**

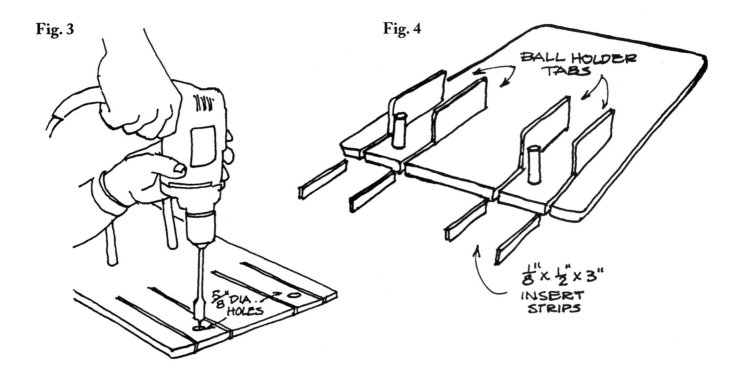

BALL HOLDER TABS

⅝" DIA. HOLES

⅛" x ½" x 3" INSERT STRIPS

There will be a gap below each of the tabs. Fill the gaps by cutting and gluing four ½x3-inch strips of scrap ⅛-inch plywood in place (see Fig. 4).

To mount the tennis equipment rack to the wall, drill a ³⁄₁₆-inch-diameter hole in each of the four cor-ners of the rack and attach it with 2½-inch #6 screws and wall anchors.

To protect the surface of the wood, cover it with three coats of a clear waterborne acrylic urethane fin-ish, sanding between coats with 220-grit sandpaper.

Ball Rack

THIS SIMPLE PROJECT requires no cutting plan, since it is constructed from one piece of 1x10 pine, with wooden dowels supporting each ball. We designed our ball rack to hold a basketball, soccer ball, volleyball, football, softball, hard ball and squash ball. When taking your measurements, design your rack to accommodate whatever sporting equipment you use most often. The ball rack can be screwed to a wall, the back of a closet door or simply leaned against a wall in a shed, garage or mud room. It's a wonderful solution for gathering together all those loose balls that otherwise are so easily misplaced.

Lay the 48-inch-long piece of 1x10 pine on a work surface and draw a line lengthwise down the center of the board. Starting 2½ inches from the bottom, temporarily arrange the balls for your board, centering

each one over the line, and placing the largest ball at the bottom. Use a pencil to make two marks, one on either side of each ball, where the dowels should go. **NOTE:** The dowels should be positioned a little less than the diameter of each ball (see Fig. 1). Allow a 1-inch space between each ball. Keep in mind that a ⅝-inch-diameter dowel will take up ⁵⁄₁₆ inch on either side of the mark.

If your selection of balls is the same as ours, lay out your board following the dimensions shown in Fig. 2; otherwise, adjust your dimensions accordingly. Use a carpenter's square to make a line through each set of marks, making sure that each line is parallel to the top and bottom of the rack (see Fig. 3).

When drilling the holes for the dowels, it is important that all the dowels be at the same 15-degree angle. You can do this by using a drill press with an adjustable

---

MATERIALS LIST

Quantity	Size	Description	Location or Use
1	48 inches	1x10 #2 pine	back panel
2	30 inches	⅝-inch-diameter wood dowels	ball holder pegs
4	2½-inch	#10 drywall screws	mounting screws
4	#6-8	plastic wall anchors	
1 bottle	8 ounces	carpenter's glue	
1 sheet	60-grit	sandpaper	
1 sheet	120-grit	sandpaper	
1 sheet	220-grit	sandpaper	
1 pint		clear waterborne acrylic urethane wood finish	

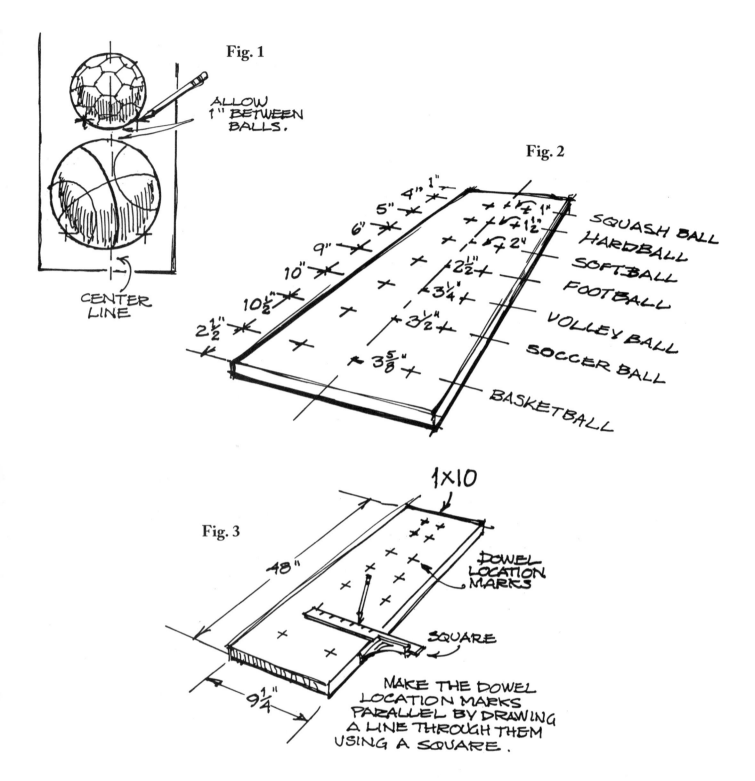

Fig. 1

ALLOW 1" BETWEEN BALLS.

CENTER LINE

Fig. 2

4" 1"
5"
6"
9"
10"
10½"
2½"

¼" 1"
¼" 1½"
¼" 2"
2½"
3¼"
3½"
3⅝"

SQUASH BALL
HARDBALL
SOFTBALL
FOOTBALL
VOLLEY BALL
SOCCER BALL
BASKETBALL

Fig. 3

1×10

48"

9¼"

DOWEL LOCATION MARKS

SQUARE

MAKE THE DOWEL LOCATION MARKS PARALLEL BY DRAWING A LINE THROUGH THEM USING A SQUARE.

tilt table or by making a jig to act as a guide when drilling the holes. For the jig, use a piece of scrap 2x4 to make several trial holes until you drill one that is exactly at a 15-degree angle. Place a dowel in the hole and use a protractor and a square to check for accuracy (see Fig. 4).

With the 2x4 jig as a guide, drill the holes by placing the jig so you can see the mark through the hole, then drill through the jig and into the 1x10 board.

Measure, mark and cut each pair of dowels to fit each ball. The dowels need to extend 1 inch past the

Fig. 4

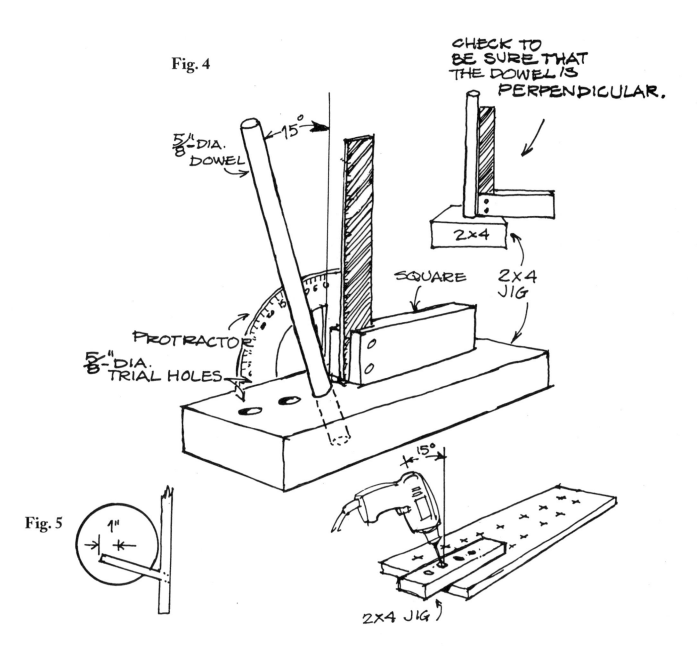

CHECK TO BE SURE THAT THE DOWEL IS PERPENDICULAR.

$\frac{5}{8}$"-DIA. DOWEL

15°

SQUARE

2×4

2×4 JIG

PROTRACTOR

$\frac{5}{8}$"-DIA. TRIAL HOLES

Fig. 5

1"

15°

2×4 JIG

widest part of the ball to be effective (see Fig. 5). Glue the pegs into the holes using carpenter's glue.

Round off the corners and edges of the backboard and sand smooth, using 60-, 120- and 220-grit sandpaper. It's a good idea to give this project several (three to four) coats of a clear waterborne acrylic urethane finish in order to protect it from the inevitable exposure to dust, dirt and fingerprints. To mount the ball rack, drill a ⅛-inch-diameter hole in each corner of the rack and screw it to a wall using 2½-inch drywall screws and wall anchors (see page 16, Attaching to the Wall).

Floor-Mounted Bike Rack

THIS BIKE RACK can be quickly and easily made from a 4x4-foot sheet of ¾-inch exterior plywood and three 6-foot-long pieces of 1x4 #2 common pine. It will accommodate any bike with wheels up to 27 inches in diameter and tires up to 2 inches wide (which includes mountain bikes). With room for four bikes, each approximately 24 inches apart, the rack can be situated outdoors, indoors or in a shed or garage. Build additional racks if you need to store more bikes.

Referring to the Cutting Plan (see Fig. 1), begin by marking the 4x4-foot sheet of ¾-inch plywood for the cuts. Use a straight board (one of the 1x4s will work well) as a straightedge to draw diagonals from corner to corner. Measure 24 inches in from each of the four corners and make a mark. Connect the marks, vertically and horizontally, to form eight equal triangles. Before cutting out the triangular pieces, use a compass to draw a 7-inch-diameter circle in the center of each of the four 24x24-inch squares.

Cut out the triangular pieces, using a portable circular saw, and then the half-circles, using an electric jigsaw.

Each bike wheel is held in place by two of the triangular plywood pieces, spaced 2 inches apart. Spacer blocks fit between each of the two triangles.

MATERIALS LIST

Quantity	Size	Description	Location or Use
1 sheet	4x4 feet	¾-inch exterior A-C plywood	vertical stands
3	6 feet	1x4 #2 common pine	cross supports
12	2 inches	1x4 #2 common pine	spacers
1 box	2-inch	galvanized finish nails	
1 box	2-inch	#8 galvanized deck screws	
1 bottle	8 ounces	waterproof glue	
1 pint		waterproof stain or preservative	

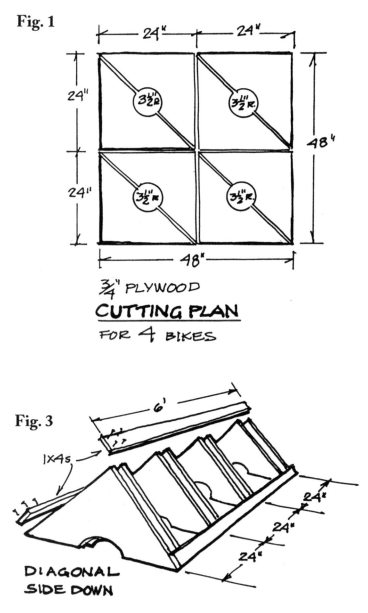

Fig. 1

24" 24"

24"

24" 48"

$3\frac{1}{2}$"R $3\frac{1}{2}$"R

$3\frac{1}{2}$"R $3\frac{1}{2}$"R

48"

$\frac{3}{4}$" PLYWOOD

CUTTING PLAN

FOR 4 BIKES

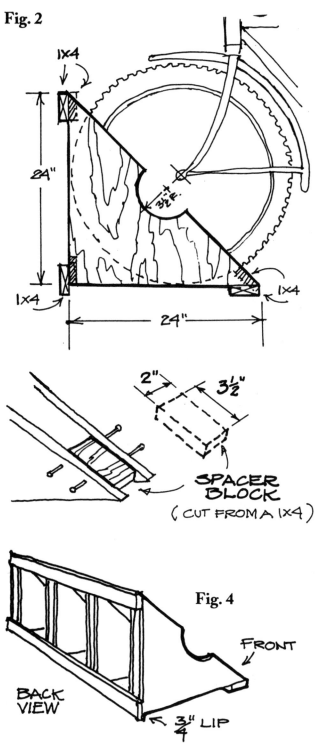

Fig. 2

1x4

24"

1x4

24"

$3\frac{1}{2}$" R.

1x4

Fig. 3

6'

1x4s

24"

24"

24"

DIAGONAL
SIDE DOWN

2" $3\frac{1}{2}$"

**SPACER
BLOCK**

(CUT FROM A 1x4)

Fig. 4

FRONT

BACK
VIEW

$\frac{3}{4}$" LIP

To make the spacers, cut 12 pieces of scrap 1x4, each 2 inches long. Glue one inside each of the three corners of each triangle. Note that the bottom front spacers are slanted to lie flush with the diagonal front edges of the triangles. For extra strength, when the glue has dried, nail 2-inch galvanized finish nails into the ends of the spacers (see Fig. 2).

After the triangular racks are glued and nailed, place them with their diagonal side down and arrange them equidistant within a 6-foot space. Screw two of the 6-foot-long 1x4s flush with the bottom edge of each triangular enclosure (see Fig. 3).

Screw the third 6-foot-long 1x4 so that it overlaps the edge by ¾ inch (see Figs. 3 and 4).

If you intend to keep the bike rack outside, we recommend giving it at least two coats of a waterproof stain or preservative.

Wall-Mounted Ski Rack

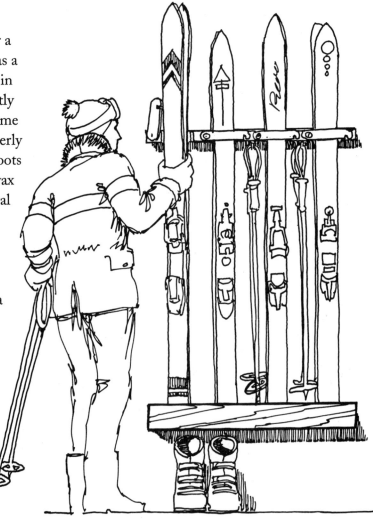

WE DISCOVERED THIS DESIGN for a ski rack while visiting a friend who has a house near the Killington Ski Center in Vermont. Although skiing equipment has greatly improved over the years, skis are still cumbersome to store. This ski rack holds your skis in an orderly fashion, allows enough space underneath for boots and has a top shelf that can hold goggles, ski wax and mittens. The rack consists of two horizontal rails mounted on the wall separately. The weight of the skis is supported by the bottom rail of the rack, while the top rail locks the skis in place. Each bar lock swings closed and is held securely by a metal angle hook resting in a slot in the bar.

Following the dimensions shown in Fig. 1, Top View, measure, mark and cut out the notches in the 2x6 top piece, using an electric jigsaw (see Fig. 2). Screw a 36-inch-long 2x4 to the back edge of the notched out 2x6, using 2½-inch galvanized deck screws spaced 6 inches apart (see Fig. 3).

MATERIALS LIST

Quantity	Size	Description	Location or Use
1	36 inches	2x6 #2 fir	top
3	36 inches	2x4 #2 fir	top & bottom
1	36 inches	1x4 #2 pine	bottom lip
1	36 inches	1x2 #2 pine	locking bars
4	1½-inch	angle hooks	catches
4	1½-inch	screw hooks	
4	2½-inch	#8 roundhead screws	
4	⅛-inch	washers	
1 box	2½-inch	#10 galvanized deck screws	
1 pint		waterproof stain or sealer	

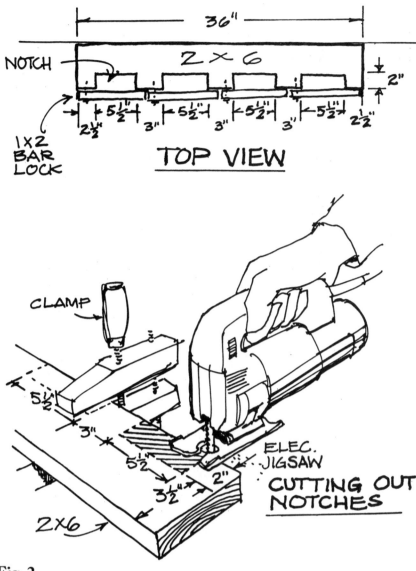

NOTCH

2 × 6

36"

2"

2¼" | 5½" | 3" | 5½" | 3" | 5½" | 3" | 5½" | 2½"

1X2 BAR LOCK

TOP VIEW

CLAMP

5½"

3"

5½"

3½"

2"

ELEC. JIGSAW

CUTTING OUT NOTCHES

2×6

Fig. 2

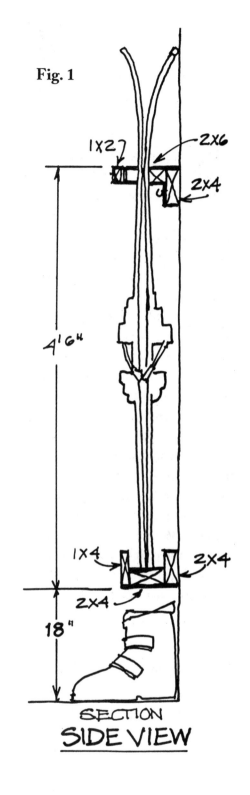

Fig. 1

1X2

2×6

2×4

4'6"

1X4

2×4

2×4

18"

SECTION SIDE VIEW

The bottom rail consists of two 36-inch-long 2x4s and one 36-inch-long 1x4, screwed together to form a "U" shape (see Fig. 1, Side View). First, screw the two 2x4s together forming a right angle, using 2½-inch galvanized deck screws placed 6 inches apart (see Fig. 4). Then screw the 36-inch-long 1x4 to the front edge of one 2x4, also using 2½-inch galvanized deck screws placed 6 inches apart.

To make the bar locks on the top rail, cut the 36-inch 1x2 into four 8½-inch pieces. Drill a ⅛-inch-diameter hole in the center of the 1x2, ¾ inch from the end (see Fig. 5). Using an electric jigsaw, cut a ¾-inch slot ¾ inch in from the other end of the 1x2.

Use the jigsaw to round off the corners of each of the four pieces.

Each bar lock is mounted to the left of one of the railing notches, using a 2½-inch roundhead screw

Fig. 3

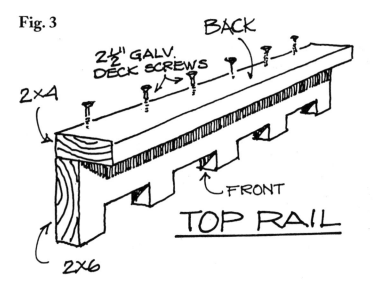

2½" GALV. DECK SCREWS

BACK

2×4

2×6

FRONT

TOP RAIL

and a ⅛-inch washer. To hold the bar lock in place, screw a 1½-inch angle hook through the slot of each bar and into the 2x6 behind it. To hold the ski poles, screw four 1½-inch screw hooks into the 2x4 back rail, each one centered between where the skis will rest (see Fig. 6). Mount the bottom rail 15 inches above the floor (to allow room for ski boots underneath), and the top rail 6 feet above the floor (see Fig. 1, Section Side View).

Protect the rack with two coats of a waterproof sealer or stain.

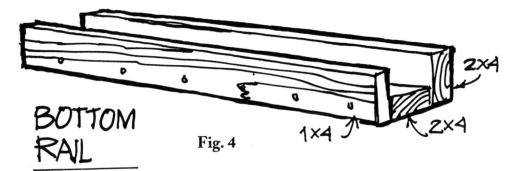

BOTTOM RAIL

Fig. 4

2×4

1×4

2×4

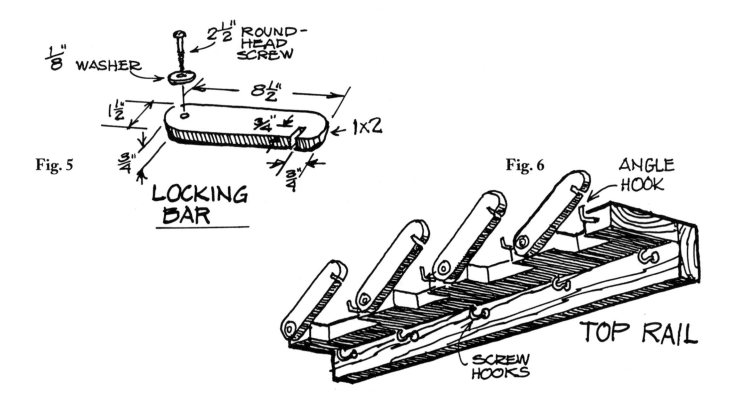

⅛" WASHER

2½" ROUND-HEAD SCREW

8½"

1½"

¾"

¾"

¾"

1×2

Fig. 5

LOCKING BAR

Fig. 6

ANGLE HOOK

SCREW HOOKS

TOP RAIL

Golf Bag Storage Unit

A FRIEND OF OURS, Bob Mathews, an avid golfer, mentioned his need for golf bag storage and suggested that we design something easy to build, that would hold golf clubs as well as golf shoes. This golf bag storage unit can be mounted on a closet door, a wall in a hallway or mudroom or in your garage. Adjust the measurements, if necessary, to fit your own equipment.

Using the dimensions shown on the Cutting Plan as your guide (see Fig. 1), begin by cutting out the pieces from the sheet of ½-inch plywood. Cut a 45-degree bevel across the top of the front and back pieces and across the bottom of the back and bottom front pieces.

To join the back and side pieces, lay the back, face side up, on a work surface. Apply glue to the outside edges of the back piece and stand the two side pieces up in position against the back piece (see Fig. 2). Before attaching the front piece of the golf storage

unit, place a bead of glue around all four edges of the inside bottom piece and slip it in place between the two side pieces.

Apply glue to the top edges of the side pieces and lay the front piece on top of the inside bottom and side pieces. Make sure that the edges of the front piece are flush with the sides, then nail the front to the sides, using 2-inch galvanized finish nails, spaced every 6 inches.

Allow the glue to set up for 20 to 30 minutes. Turn the unit on one side and nail the side pieces to the back (see Fig. 3). Turn the unit on its other side, and repeat the procedure. Then, turn it onto its back and glue and nail the bottom front piece to the sides (see Fig. 4).

Make an L-shaped shoe support by gluing and nailing together the 3x13-inch piece of plywood to the top edge of the 5x13-inch piece (see Fig. 5). Slide the shoe support into the hole provided

MATERIALS LIST

Quantity	Size	Description	Location or Use
1 sheet	4x8 feet	½-inch plywood	front, back, sides, bottom pieces, shoe support
1 box	2-inch	galvanized finish nails	
2	2½-inch	#10 panhead screws	
1 bottle	8 ounces	carpenter's glue	
1 sheet	60-grit	sandpaper	
1 sheet	120-grit	sandpaper	
1 sheet	220-grit	sandpaper	
1 pint		waterproof paint or stain	

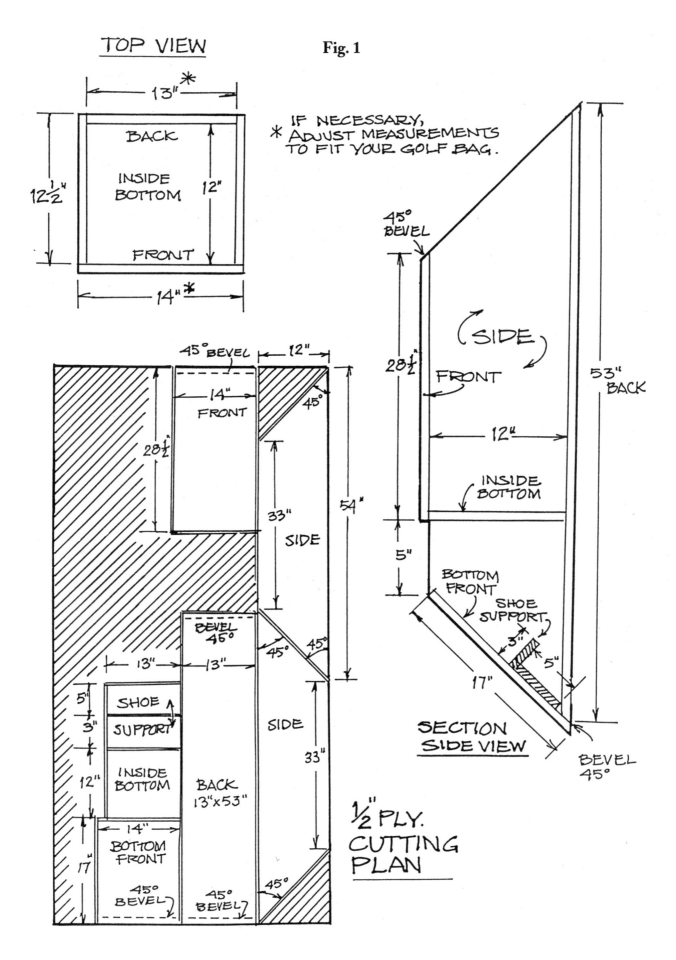

TOP VIEW   Fig. 1

13"*

BACK

INSIDE
BOTTOM   12"

FRONT

12½"

14"*

IF NECESSARY,
* ADJUST MEASUREMENTS
TO FIT YOUR GOLF BAG.

45° BEVEL   12"

14"
FRONT

28½"

33"

SIDE

54"

45°

45°

BEVEL
45°

13"   13"

5"
SHOE
3"
SUPPORT

INSIDE
BOTTOM

12"

14"

17"
BOTTOM
FRONT

45°
BEVEL

45° BEVEL

BACK
13"x53"

45°

SIDE

33"

45°

½" PLY.
CUTTING
PLAN

45°
BEVEL

SIDE

28½"

FRONT

12"

INSIDE
BOTTOM

5"

BOTTOM
FRONT

SHOE
SUPPORT

3"

5"

17"

SECTION
SIDE VIEW

53"
BACK

BEVEL
45°

Fig. 2

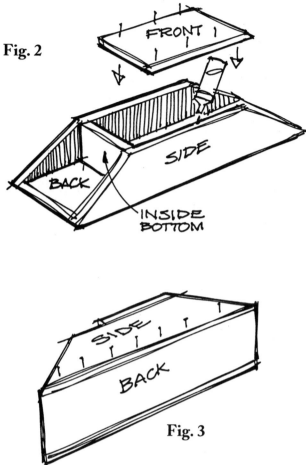

Fig. 4

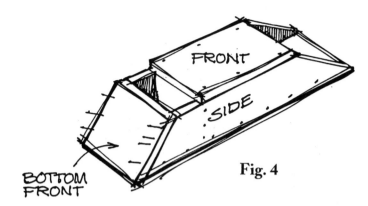

Fig. 3

Fig. 5

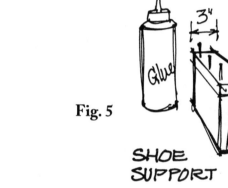

SHOE SUPPORT

at the base of the golf storage box. It is not necessary to glue it in place (see Fig. 1, Section Side View).

Sand with 60-, 120- and 220-grit sandpaper and finish with three coats of a waterproof paint or stain.

Hang the unit on a wall or door by drilling two ³/₁₆-inch-diameter holes in the upper corners of the back piece. Use two 2½-inch panhead screws to attach the unit to the wall or door (see page 16, Attaching to the Wall). For a more professional look, use finishing washers where it's mounted.

Glossary of Terms

Bar clamp: A long metal bar with an adjustable clamp.

Batten: A piece of lumber screwed across the back of doors or shutters to strengthen them.

Beveled cut: An angled cut.

Block plane: A small hand tool used to shave off or smooth lumber.

Butt hinges: Standard hinges.

Cabinet-grade plywood: Has a smooth, blemish-free face of hardwood veneer, usually birch, oak or lauan. Not suitable for outdoor exposure.

Chisel: A straight or beveled-edge tool used for paring wood or cutting out mortises.

Combination square: A 12-inch-long measuring tool with a sliding head, which can be adjusted at different lengths. The head has one edge at a 90-degree (right) angle to the blade and the other edge at a 45-degree angle.

Counterbore: To bore a hole in order to recess a screw head. The hole is often filled with a wooden plug.

Countersink: To bore a conical hole so that a screw head can lie flush with the surface of the wood.

Crosscut: A cut running perpendicular to the grain of the wood.

Dado: A rectangular groove cut in a board.

Electric jigsaw (or saber saw): An electric portable saw used to make curved cuts.

Exterior plywood (ext. ply.): Plywood in which the plies are bonded together using exterior or waterproof glue. Commonly available in face grades of A, B and C.

Finish nail: A slender nail with a small cupped head, which can be driven beneath the surface of the wood with a nail set.

Framing square (or carpenter's square): A 24-inch by 16-inch L-shaped measuring tool for laying out lines. The body or long member is 2 inches wide and the tongue is 1½ inches wide. It is used to check for square on large stock.

Kerf: The groove made by the cut of a saw blade or the width of the cut itself.

Lag screw (or lag bolt): A large screw with a hexagonal head that is used to join heavy pieces of lumber.

Lap joint: A joint made by lapping one piece of wood over another.

Miter: An angled cut, usually 45 degrees.

Mitered cut: Used to crosscut lumber when making trim or cutting narrow pieces of stock less than 6 inches wide. A wood miter box can make 45- or 90-degree cuts.

Molding: A strip of wood with a curved surface, used for decorative purposes.

Mortise: A notch cut in a piece of wood to receive a protruding part.

Nail set: A small tool used to hammer nail heads beneath the wood's surface.

Nominal size: Size of lumber by which it is commonly known and sold (not the actual size).

On-center (O.C.): The distance from the center of one piece of lumber to the center of another.

Piano hinge (or continuous hinge): Extends the entire length of the two pieces of wood to be hinged together.

Phillips screwdriver bit: An attachment for an electric drill used to drive Phillips-head (cross-head) screws.

Pilot hole: A hole, slightly smaller than the nail shaft or screw thread, drilled into a piece of wood to help guide a nail or screw and to prevent splitting.

Plumb: Exactly vertical. Can be checked using a level.

Pressure-treated lumber (P.T. or C.C.A. lumber): Lumber that has been chemically treated to resist rot and insects.

Rabbet: A cut made in the edge of a board when constructing a joint.

Rasp: A rough-edged file with triangular teeth, used to shape wood when a lot of material must be removed.

Rip cut: A cut made parallel to the direction of the wood grain.

Router: An electric tool used to cut grooves and shape lumber into various molding profiles.

Section: A drawing that shows the "cut-through" view of a building or object.

Spade drill bit: A flat drill used for making ⅜-inch- to 1½-inch-diameter holes in wood.

Speed square: A triangular-shaped metal tool used as a guide for cutting lumber at right angles with an electric saw.

Stud: Lumber used for the vertical framing members in a wall.

Toe-nail: To drive a nail at an angle.

Tongue-and-groove (T&G): Boards in which the tongue of one board fits into the groove of another.

Trim: Decorative molding used to cover joints.

Twist drill bit: A durable high-speed drill used to drill small holes from 1⁄16 inch to 1½ inches in diameter.

Utility knife: A thin-bladed cutting tool used to cut shingles and other thin building materials.

Veneer: A thin sheet of wood. Veneers are glued together in layers to make plywood.

Wood clamp (or hand screw): Two wooden jaws with adjustable threaded steel rods running through them.

Wood putty: Used to fill nail holes, gaps and defects in wood.

Sources

TOOLS

Bench Table Saw
Harbor Freight Tools
3491 Mission Oaks Blvd.
Camarillo, CA 93011-6010
800-423-2567

Clamps
Woodworker's Warehouse
135 American Legion Hwy.
Revere, MA 02151
617-286-5200

Electric Woodburning Tool
Woodcraft
210 Wood County Industrial Park
P.O. Box 1686
Parkersburg, WV 26102-1686
304-422-5412

Featherboard
Woodworker's Supply
1108 N. Glenn Rd.
Casper, WY 82601
800-645-9292

HARDWARE

Casters
Woodworker's Supply
1108 N. Glenn Rd.
Casper, WY 82601
800-645-9292

Hasps & Hinges
Artesanos Imports Co., Inc.
222 Galisteo St.
Santa Fe, NM 87501
505-983-5563

Kraft Hardware
306 E. 61st St.
New York, NY 10021
212-838-2214

Lid Support
Woodworker's Warehouse
135 American Legion Hwy.
Revere, MA 02151
800-818-8652

Index

Storage Projects You Can Build

About the Authors

JAMES STILES

DAVID STILES is a designer/builder and illustrator, and the author of eight other how-to books, including *Sheds* and *The Treehouse Book* (which won the ALA Notable Children's Book Award). A graduate of Pratt Institute and The Academy of Fine Arts in Florence, Italy, he is the winner of two awards from the New York Planning Commission. His articles have appeared in *House Beautiful*, *Country Journal*, *HomeMechanix* and the *New York Times*.

JEAN TRUSTY STILES, a graduate of Wheaton College, lives in New York City, where she is an actress/model and an instructor of English as a Second Language. Jeanie and David have written *Playhouses You Can Build*, *Kids' Furniture You Can Build*, *Garden Projects* and *Woodworking Simplified* and have appeared on numerous television programs, including the "Our Home" and "Handmade by Design" shows. They have a 22-year-old daughter, Lief Anne, who recently graduated from Duke University, and divide their time between New York City and East Hampton, New York.